GREG L. HAWKINS AND CALLY PARKINSON

WITH CONTRIBUTIONS FROM ERIC ARNSON   FOREWORD BY BILL HYBELS

REV

WHERE ARE YOU?

BILL HYBELS

Founding and Senior Pastor
Willow Creek Community Church

Chairman of the Board
Willow Creek Association

FOREWORD

The local church is the hope of the world.

For a number of years now, I have shared this message whenever I've had the opportunity to serve pastors of local churches across the nation and around the world. It's a message I believe with all my heart.

So you can imagine my reaction when three people whose counsel I value told me that the local church I've been the pastor of for more than three decades was not doing as well as we thought when it came to spiritual growth.

As if that wasn't bad enough, they said this wasn't just their opinion. It was based on scientific research.

Ouch.

Led by staff members Greg Hawkins and Cally Parkinson, and consumer research advisor Eric Arnson, we began our 2004 congregational survey looking through a new set of lenses. Thanks to Eric's ideas and counsel, the survey allowed us to utilize some of the most advanced research methods available.

This team brings much to the table. Eric is one of the smartest men I've ever met, with humility to match. Cally, who at the time was Willow's communications director, ran point on the project. I learned early on that I could count on her to make things happen. Greg, Willow Creek's executive pastor, provided leadership for this whole process. After eleven years of working with Greg, I can't imagine doing ministry without him by my side.

They convinced me that through this research, we could gain a unique understanding of the spiritual lives of our people—how they grow and what we can do to help them.

Some of the data from the study revealed encouraging signs of vitality. For example, 50 percent of the congregation indicated they "loved God more than anything else" and were expressing that love

When I first heard these results, the pain of knowing was almost unbearable. Upon reflection, I realized that the pain of not knowing could be catastrophic.

by reaching out to their unchurched friends and serving the poor on a regular basis. However, other parts of the research did not shine brightly on our church. Among the findings: nearly one out of every four people at Willow Creek were stalled in their spiritual growth or dissatisfied with the church—and many of them were considering leaving.

When I first heard these results, the pain of knowing was almost unbearable. Upon reflection, I realized that the pain of not knowing could be catastrophic.

What you hold in your hands has revolutionized the way I look at the role of the local church. It is causing me to ask new questions. It is causing me to rethink how we coach Christ-followers. It is causing me to see clearly that the church and its myriad of programs have taken on too much of the responsibility for people's spiritual growth.

On these pages, Greg, Cally, and Eric share the heart and the understanding that have gone into this ongoing project, and the results and the insights that have come from it thus far. They will encourage you to take steps to better support the spiritual growth of the people in your church.

At the end of the day, the discoveries in this book have made me even more committed to continue learning—and working hard—to ensure that our church is reaching its full redemptive potential. I hope you'll join with me. My prayer is that this information begins an ongoing dialogue about spiritual growth in *your* church.

My challenge to you is this: Be open to hearing God speak to you as you read these pages. I've learned over the years that it's imperative to face the facts. Facts are your friends—challenging friends, yet friends nonetheless.

Bill Hybels

Bill Hybels

My challenge to you is this: Be open to hearing God speak to you as you read these pages.

PREVIEW

Greg L. Hawkins

Every ministry leader wants to make an impact. But how do we know if the things we are doing as a church actually make a difference? We can measure things like membership and attendance, but do these measures really tell us whether or not someone is becoming more like Christ? How do we measure the human heart?

Greg L. Hawkins

Needing to set a new strategic course, Willow Creek began by asking, "Where are we?" The church gained a much deeper understanding of the answer to this question by utilizing a unique research method. The results were surprising.

Cally Parkinson

The results of three years of research designed to measure how people grow spiritually revealed a great deal about the path individuals follow on their spiritual journeys, the unique needs they have along the way and how the church has met—and failed to meet—those needs. Six provocative discoveries provide the springboard for churches to reconsider ministry strategies.

4 **So What Can You Do Now?**
Greg L. Hawkins

After considering all the data and discoveries, it's fair to ask, "So what?" It's also essential to wrestle with tough questions and begin to take action. Three next-step ideas help leaders and churches who are ready to address the question, "Where are we?"

Afterword: Where Are *You?*
Greg L. Hawkins

Appendices

Eric Arnson

Eric Arnson

Cally Parkinson

WHERE ARE YOU?

God's kingdom is like seed thrown on a field by a man who then goes to bed and forgets about it. The seed sprouts and grows—he has no idea how it happens. *Mark 4:26–27 (MSG)*

✦

For as long as anyone can remember, the only question we knew to ask about the church was, "How many?"

But "How many?"—*by itself*—doesn't completely address what the church is called to do. That question is a good start, but it measures only what we see.

When it comes to spiritual growth, we need to be able to measure the unseen. We need a glimpse of people's attitudes, thoughts and feelings. We need words that reveal the heart of each person. We want to know what moves them at the deepest levels.

We need a fresh view. We need another question. We need a question that helps us understand the spiritual journey so we can help and encourage people in their pursuit of Christ.

The question is simple, but we continually push it away. It's the central question between God and us.

And God was the first one to ask it:

Thousands of people have told us about their relationship with God. We've listened with no other goal than to see how God works in people's lives. When we look at the results, we see patterns. The research is scientific. The patterns are biblical.

The insights provide a context to answer the question "Where are you?" for every person pursuing Christ.

The health of your church is not just about the numbers. It's about the movement of people toward Christ, toward deep love for God and genuine love for others.

Where are the people who attend your services? Are they moving closer to God? What if you could know? What if you could see?

Where are you?

The answer is revealing. It's God's question to each of us. We're just joining the conversation.

We need a fresh view. We need another question.

GREG L. HAWKINS

REVEAL

1 **ARE YOU *REALLY*
MAKING A DIFFERENCE?**

**THE BRUTAL TRUTH
ABOUT SPIRITUAL
GROWTH**

kingdom
impact

EVERY MINISTRY LEADER wants to make an impact. But how do we know if the things we are doing as a church actually make a difference? We can measure things like membership and attendance, but do these measures really tell us whether or not someone is becoming more like Christ? How do we measure the human heart?

(1)

ARE YOU *REALLY* MAKING A DIFFERENCE?

A new member of your church has asked to meet you for lunch. After some small talk, he looks you in the eye and says, "My wife and I want to do something for the church. We'd like to donate one million dollars."

Did I hear that right? One million dollars?

"Excuse me?" is the best response you can offer.

Again he says, "We'd like to give the church one million dollars. The only thing we ask . . ."

Oh no, here come the attached strings . . .

". . . is that you put the money toward what you know will result in the greatest kingdom impact. We want you to guarantee that people far from God will be found and that the found will grow in their love for God and other people."

A thousand ideas run through your head. With that kind of money, you could do just about anything and everything you can think of—buy land, build buildings, hire staff, pay down debt, fund mission trips, launch a regional campus.

It would be great if you could look your new friend in the eye and say, "I know exactly how to invest that money to guarantee the greatest kingdom impact." But we all know we can't make a guarantee like that. The thought alone is crazy.

Why?

Because we know God—and God alone—changes a human life. As we're taught in Philippians 2:13, "for it is God who works in you to will and to act according to his good purpose" (NIV). How he does that is mysterious and unknowable. And it's unique to every person. The way God has worked to change my life is different than how he has worked to change your life.

God—and God alone—changes a human life.

But let's get back to the million-dollar gift. Imagine there was no "guarantee clause" attached. What if your new friend just slid the check across the table and said, "Invest it wisely"?

What would you do with the money?

THE BRUTAL TRUTH

If you're like me, you would do what church leaders have been doing for generations: design and fund an assortment of church activities and programs that you sincerely believe will help people grow spiritually.

Then you'd encourage as many people as possible to get involved in those activities and programs, believing that increased participation means the lost are being reached and believers are growing (see Illustration 1-1: "The Church Activity Model for Spiritual Growth"). And, conversely, decreased participation means people aren't being reached and aren't growing.

The Church Activity Model for Spiritual Growth

A person far from God
participates in church activities
which produce a person who loves God and loves others.

Illustration 1-1: Many churches work from a model similar to this: the more a person far from God participates in church activities, the more likely it is those activities will produce a person who loves God and loves others.

But let's stop and really think that through. Does increased attendance in ministry programs *automatically* equate to spiritual growth?

To be brutally honest: it does not.

Attendance numbers help you determine if people like what you are doing. If they like what's happening, they choose to participate. (Conversely, if they don't like what's happening, they choose not to participate.) Maybe they like the music, or perhaps they appreciate how you are helping their children. Maybe they are making new friends. Perhaps they appreciate the opportunities provided to help others.

The hope is that whatever draws them in helps them to experience the transforming power of God and as a result to grow spiritually.

But the bottom line is that attendance numbers alone will never provide the information we need in order to know conclusively that church activities are really helping people grow. Attendance is one measure that something is working, but it is not the whole story.

Here's the problem.

When it comes to numbers, we as leaders start to actually believe that attendance is the only thing we need to look at. It becomes a simple equation: *increased attendance = people growing*.

It's a whole lot easier to count heads than it is to measure hearts.

We're not poor leaders when we think like this; it's just that we don't have any other practical way to measure growth. It's a whole lot easier to count heads than it is to measure heart change. Trust me, I know.

Looking back over my sixteen years on staff at Willow Creek Community Church, I have witnessed numbers regularly increasing. I have been part of a leadership team that has seen our church grow more than 50 percent in attendance. Participation in small groups has increased by 500 percent, and we have witnessed a dramatic increase in the number of people who serve the poor.

I see increased numbers, but I also see more than numbers. I know that God is at work in our ministry because I see life change—and I hear story after story about how God is using our church to make a difference in life after life.

At the end of most days, I'm excited about what I see and what I've been privileged to be part of as a leader. I feel like I have followed God's leadings, and he has been faithful to show our team what we should be doing.

But then there are nights I lie in bed and I wonder.

I wonder if we could be doing something different or better. I wonder if we are investing people's time and money in the most effective way. I wonder if we're really making a difference. And I wonder if my motivation is more about seeing numbers grow and less about seeing hearts grow. After all, if the numbers are growing, then all my hard work and sacrifice are not in vain.

Right?

FINDING A WAY
TO MEASURE HEARTS

One of my kids' favorite stories (and mine too) is *How the Grinch Stole Christmas* by Dr. Seuss. If you remember the story, the Grinch is a grouch. No one really knows why he is the way he is, but the storyteller would lead us to believe that perhaps his heart is two sizes too small.

How do we know that? Well, when we watch the animated movie, there is a magic X-ray screen that shows us that indeed the Grinch's heart *is* two sizes too small. Fortunately, that's not the end of the story. After doing a lot of really bad stuff to the town of Whoville (and poor Cindy Lou Who), the Grinch has a life-changing experience. We actually get to *see* the transformation of his heart. Thanks again to that magic screen, we watch as the Grinch's heart grows three sizes that Christmas day!

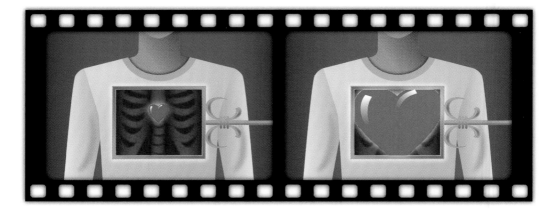

We may have found a new tool to help you get a clearer picture of the hearts of your people.

If we had access to Dr. Seuss's research labs, we could measure heart change like that to really see if a person's heart for God and others is growing. Then we could learn what the church is doing to help the spiritual growth process. We would have a better idea of how best to spend our time and our resources. We would know which ministries to start, which ones to change and which ones to shut down altogether. We would know for sure if we're really making a difference.

And we would be more confident to spend any surprise million-dollar gifts that come our way. We might not be able to provide a guarantee (only God can do that), but we could sleep a whole lot better at night knowing we were wise stewards with that gift.

It is too bad that we don't have a magic X-ray machine like that, so we could find out if what we're doing as a church is *really* making a difference.

This might surprise you, but we think we might have discovered something along these lines. No, we didn't get access to Dr. Seuss's lab, but we believe we may have found a new tool that might be able to help you get a clearer picture of the hearts of your people.

Sound intriguing? In the pages that follow, we'll give you some background on how we discovered this tool, and then we'll dive in to what we discovered as a result. Read on!

GREG L. HAWKINS

REVEAL

2 **WHAT HAPPENED WHEN WILLOW
ASKED, "WHERE ARE WE?"**

SURPRISING RESEARCH
FINDINGS THAT
ROCKED WILLOW

"Now what?"

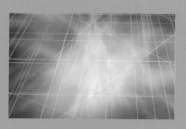

NEEDING TO SET A NEW STRATEGIC COURSE, Willow Creek began by asking, "Where are we?" The church gained a much deeper understanding of the answer to this question by utilizing a unique research method. The results were surprising.

WHAT HAPPENED WHEN WILLOW ASKED, "WHERE ARE WE?"

Ministry is often an uphill battle. You're following God's call with your life, but the day-to-day battles leave you wondering which way is up. Then there are times when you feel God's hand so directly on your ministry that you sense *this* is what Moses must have experienced when he was atop the mountain with God. And, of course, there are those times when there's very little separating the mountaintop experiences from the uphill battles!

Back in the fall of 2003, Willow was in the midst of a mountaintop season. We were one year away from opening a new 7,200-seat auditorium. Yet I knew that after all the excitement of the grand opening had passed (and people had figured out where they wanted to sit), they would soon start asking, "Now what? How are we going to use this beautiful new space to reach our community and impact our world?" Because they had sacrificed and donated tens of millions of dollars to the cause, their question seemed pretty reasonable to me.

In anticipation of that question, we knew it was time for some strategic planning. We needed to understand what God wanted our church to do over the next several years, and strategic planning is a helpful tool that had served us well before. So we moved forward, engaging the senior staff, the elders and the board of directors in a highly collaborative process.

We knew it was time for some strategic planning.

three questions

When we do strategic planning, I have found it useful to organize our work around three simple but profound questions:

- *Where are we?*

- *What do we see?*

- *How do we get there?*

Where are we?   Before we looked to the future, we needed to step back and tell ourselves the truth about what was really going on in our church and in our community. We needed to grapple with honest answers to questions like, How well are we achieving our mission? Why do people come to the church? Why do people leave? What is our distinct competency—the one thing we do best now? What are our financial and facility realities? What are the pressing needs of our community and extended region? We needed to define our **Current Reality.**

What do we see?   Specifically, we needed to ask, What do we see in the future? What do we all sense God wants to do through our church over the next five years? What picture of the future ignites everyone's passion? We needed a clear **Vision.**

How do we get there?   Only after we were clear about our current reality and our vision could we answer this question. We needed to determine the specific actions that would help us bridge the gap between where we were and where we wanted to go. We needed to define the specific strategies we would embrace, and we needed to declare our priorities in order to allot our resources wisely. We needed an **Action Plan.**

Before we looked to the future, we needed to step back and tell ourselves the truth.

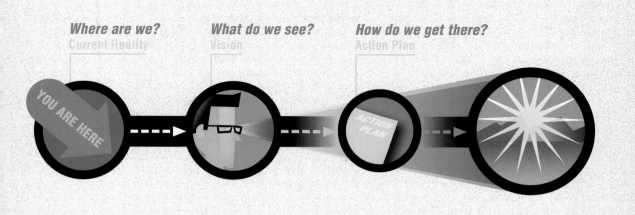

Where are we?
Current Reality

What do we see?
Vision

How do we get there?
Action Plan

YOU ARE HERE

ACTION PLAN

GAINING INSIGHTS

So we began with the first question, "Where are we?" to get a handle on what was really going on in our church. To answer the question accurately, we knew we needed more than everyone's best opinions about what was really working and not working in our church. We needed congregational research.

We did our first research in 1992 and have continued to survey our entire congregation every three years or so to learn all sorts of things. We want to know why people come to our church in the first place. We want to know which programs and activities they are involved in. We want to know where they live so we can figure out our impact in the various communities around the church.

Over the years, the insights from these surveys have shaped—and reshaped—our thinking, directly influencing our plans. For example, in 1995 we discovered that one-third of our congregation drove more than thirty minutes to attend our services. We learned that these people were not inviting their unchurched neighbors and friends to services, nor were they significantly involved in other strategic ministries. Basically, we discovered that more than 30 percent of our congregation did not participate in our mission of turning irreligious people into fully devoted followers of Jesus Christ.

We began with the first question, "Where are we?" to get a handle on what was really going on in our church.

That sobering view of a current reality forced us to ask some hard questions. Do we plant new churches closer to these folks? Do we encourage them to attend a church closer to where they live? Do we do nothing and just be glad they are going to church somewhere? There were no easy answers, and we wrestled with this issue for several years. Finally, in 2000, we moved forward with plans to launch a regional ministry strategy that has thus far resulted in four additional campuses with more than five thousand people who now attend church closer to their home. Without the foundation of this research, I am convinced our strategic planning would never have gone in this direction.

A NEW INSIGHT, A NEW APPROACH

That brings us back to the fall of 2003 with a new auditorium springing up from our parking lot and the need for a fresh vision looming even larger. I knew we needed to do research to jumpstart our strategic planning process. I had done this type of research before and I thought I knew what to expect, but God had something—or rather, someone—completely different in mind.

"Is there anything else going on in your ministry you think I should know about?"

One day I was wrapping up a meeting with Cally Parkinson, our new communications director. I decided to ask her one last question before she left my office. Given the fast-paced ministry demands I was juggling, it was hard to stay up on all that was going on. I had learned that I occasionally stumble onto something important if I just ask this simple question: "Is there anything else going on in your ministry you think I should know about?"

Cally responded by saying, "As a matter of fact, there is."

She told me that when she was an executive with Allstate Insurance, she had hired Eric Arnson to do some consulting. Eric's groundbreaking research helped Allstate understand what was happening in the hearts and minds of their existing and potential customers. Cally told me that Eric had just left McKinsey & Company, a management consulting firm where he had been a partner. I had spent five years with McKinsey prior to joining the staff at Willow, so I was intrigued.

"Maybe Eric could help us with our upcoming research," Cally said. That ended up being the understatement of a lifetime.

Relying on Eric's world-class experience, we embarked on what would become a three-year process of study and research that included:

- A 2004 analysis of 6000 surveys completed by people who attend Willow Creek.

- A 2004 analysis of 300 surveys completed by people who left Willow Creek within the previous year.

- A 2007 analysis of 5000 surveys completed by congregants who attend Willow Creek and six other churches across the United States. These churches represent a small sample of all churches, but cover both independent and denominational churches and represent geographic, age and cultural diversity.

- More than 120 in-depth one-on-one conversations (conducted in 2004 and 2007) with people in which we explored their spiritual lives.

- Study of Scripture and more than one hundred books and articles on spiritual formation and human development.

- Consultation with experts in the area of spiritual growth.

It has caused us to rethink everything about how we do church.

Eric's unique analytical approach allowed us to dig much deeper than we've ever been able to do before using our traditional research methods. (For more information, see "Is It Possible to Measure the Heart?" on pages 25-26). And it resulted in insights we've never had before. In fact, the results were so startling that our strategic planning process slowed down considerably just to allow us to assimilate the findings.

For three years, we have wrestled at the most senior levels of our church with what this research is revealing to us. It has caused us to rethink *everything* about how we do church. We have pushed at the research conclusions and have found them to be solid.

In the following pages, we want to share with you what we've discovered. We believe that what we're learning is too important to keep to ourselves.

And to think it all began with asking the question, "Where are we?"

Eric Arnson | # Is It Possible to (Measure the Heart?)

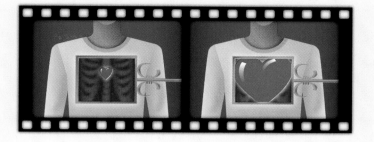

AS A CONSUMER RESEARCH EXPERT, I am dedicated to developing insights into consumers in order to increase product sales. I use scientific methods to look beyond surface characteristics such as gender, race, age and income. Instead, I delve into the deeper issues—emotions, motivations and needs—that drive consumers to choose one product over another. In other words, I measure the unseen realities, or intangibles, that cause people to buy what they buy.

When Greg mentioned that he'd like to have a tool that could measure the heart (like the Grinch's X-ray machine), he was talking about this research approach that focuses on people's emotions and attitudes. In the marketplace, we've found that looking at consumers through this type of lens is far more powerful than mere demographics because it creates a much stronger measure of something we researchers call "predictiveness."

Predictiveness is the degree to which we can predict whether or not someone is likely to behave a certain way or to try a new product. This is logical. How people *feel* about something influences how they *act*. The measures we use are self-descriptive; we ask how strongly consumers feel about things by measuring the strength of their response (for example, *strongly agree, agree, disagree*, etc.). In our spiritual growth survey, we asked how strongly people felt about statements like "I love God more than anything" and "I have tremendous love for people I know and don't know" to gauge the level of people's emotional commitment to their faith.

But just measuring emotions and attitudes (how strongly people feel about things) is not what makes this work unique. What makes this approach so powerful is that we are able to compare and correlate attitudinal responses (like those above) with behavioral responses. In our spiritual growth survey, we asked people behavioral questions about things like serving at the church, Bible study, attendance at services, small groups, prayer, solitude—even how they used the Internet in their spiritual life.

A high correlation between attitudes and behaviors is called *predictiveness*. In our work on spiritual growth, we were on the hunt for the attitudes and behaviors that would form a directly related set of "segments" (groups of people with common characteristics). Then we looked through that lens at another set of very important questions about what people want from their church. For example, we asked them to rate their levels of satisfaction with the church in response to statements like "helps me understand the Bible in greater depth" or "helps me feel like I belong." Based on their responses, we were able to develop maybe the most critical finding of all—an understanding of what people *need* to advance their spiritual growth.

continued on next page

Is It Possible to (Measure the Heart?)

That's the formula for our version of the Grinch's magic X-ray machine: attitudes/emotions + behaviors = segments of people with unique sets of needs. With this kind of ability to understand what might capture people's minds and hearts, a church's ability to make effective strategic choices about how to spend time and resources improves dramatically.

The chart below contrasts a marketplace example and a church-related example that may make this concept easier to understand.

In our ongoing work on spiritual growth, we want to go beyond merely understanding the specific needs of individual segments. We hope we can identify opportunities for new church initiatives and ministry activities specifically designed to *catalyze growth* along the spiritual journey. This a key difference between the objectives of the church and the typical goals for a business. In the marketplace, a business wants to find a great target market segment and serve it very well. In the church, we want to do whatever we can to initiate movement from one segment of spiritual growth to the next. ✦

CHART 2-1   **Measuring the Heart in the Marketplace and in the Church**

THE SEGMENT	ATTITUDES / EMOTIONS + BEHAVIORS	POTENTIAL NEEDS	POTENTIAL UNDERMET OR UNMET NEEDS
A consumer in the marketplace: for example, a dedicated amateur athlete	• *Cares a great deal about what he/she eats and drinks* • *Wants to maximize, not compromise, athletic performance with what he/she eats and drinks*	*Replenishing fluids to sustain performance during sporting events*	*Healthy high-performance drink*
An individual in the church: for example, a Christ-Centered believer	• *Enjoys volunteering; sees serving as a way of life* • *Experiences tremendous love for God and others*	*A wide range of challenging serving opportunities*	*Opportunities to coach or mentor others on their spiritual journey*

CALLY PARKINSON

REV

❸ WHAT DID WE DISCOVER?

SIX PROVOCATIVE DISCOVERIES
THAT WILL CHANGE THE
WAY YOU THINK

THE RESULTS OF THREE YEARS of research designed to measure how people grow spiritually revealed a great deal about the path individuals follow on their spiritual journeys, the unique needs they have along the way and how the church has met—and failed to meet—those needs. Six provocative discoveries provide the springboard for churches to reconsider ministry strategies.

3

WHAT DID WE DISCOVER?

Our research goal was daunting, but simple. We wanted to find evidence of spiritual growth in people, and then figure out what types of activities or circumstances triggered that spiritual growth.

An increasing love for God and for other people was our working definition of spiritual growth. We based this definition on Jesus' description of the two greatest commandments: "'You must love the Lord your God with all your heart, all your soul, and all your mind.' This is the first and greatest commandment. A second is equally important: 'Love your neighbor as yourself'" (Matthew 22:37–39 NLT). We took that to mean that spiritual growth occurs as one's love for God and for others increases.

In pursuit of our goal, we spent three years digesting research and analysis based on 2.6 million data points from more than eleven thousand completed surveys. That includes data from Willow Creek and six additional churches. The six churches are diverse in geographic location and size, ranging from larger churches in Florida and California; to suburban churches in Illinois, Ohio and Texas; to a smaller, predominantly African-American church in Michigan. They included denominational, seeker-targeted and independent/ Bible churches.

We wanted to find evidence of spiritual growth in people, and then figure out what types of activities or circumstances triggered that spiritual growth.

HOW WE BEGAN

The first step in any research project is to develop a hypothesis—a theory about what you think you'll discover. Much like a good detective, a researcher looks for clues in many different places to shape the direction of the work. Hypotheses help determine the questions to ask, and they guide the analysis of data.

We developed our hypotheses using data from previous Willow Creek congregational studies, plus input from more than 120 one-on-one interviews with people who attend the church. We also evaluated emerging trends in the church world, such as the growing popularity of postmodern churches and the movement away from offering separate seeker- and believer-targeted services.

With all of this background information and analysis, we headed into the research with three hypotheses to guide us:

1. *There is a migration path for spiritual growth based on church activities.*

2. *The most effective evangelism tool is a spiritual conversation.*

3. *Spiritual relationships are a key driver of spiritual growth.*

Hypothesis 1: *There is a migration path for spiritual growth based on church activities.*

We hypothesized that spiritual growth depended on increasing participation in church activities such as small groups, serving, midweek believer services (in addition to weekend seeker services) and Bible study groups. In other words, our hypothesis was that the more involved people are in the church, the closer they grow to Christ. We also suspected there were two main barriers to spiritual growth: time/schedule conflicts that prevented participation in church activities, and a lack of overall effectiveness in small groups.

Hypothesis 2: *The most effective evangelism tool is a spiritual conversation.*

One-on-one interviews led us to our next hypothesis: Having spiritual conversations with seekers is the most effective strategy for personal evangelism, and there are many different communication styles that work in evangelistic outreach. We believed that putting increased emphasis on spiritual conversations and recognizing multiple evangelistic styles would increase the congregation's desire to be personally involved in reaching out to seekers.

Hypothesis 3: *Spiritual relationships are a key driver of spiritual growth.*

Our past research indicated that people looked to small groups for deep spiritual relationships. However, we kept hearing in our one-on-one interviews that people felt something was missing from the small group experience. We knew we needed to better understand the effectiveness of small groups in helping facilitate this need for connection.

Our hypothesis was that the more involved people are in the church, the closer they grow to Christ.

We fielded an electronic survey based on the most advanced research methods available.

Guided by these three hypotheses, we fielded an electronic survey based on the most advanced research methods available. This included the extensive qualitative work (in-depth one-on-one interviews), professional survey design and data analysis by the world's largest custom market research firm. In addition, through Eric Arnson's contacts, we were able to benefit from independent analyses by multiple research veterans, plus a third-party assessment from an international research group.

We're about to dive into the results of the research, but keep these three hypotheses in mind; we'll circle back to them later to assess whether or not they were on target.

WHAT WE DID NOT FIND

Before revealing what we did find, it's important to include three key observations about what we *did not* find.

Observation | **1**

Gender *does not* impact spiritual growth in any significant way. We did have a female bias in the sample, which means more women than men participated. But the differences between male and female responses to virtually every question in the survey were surprisingly small. This means the research findings are statistically gender-blind and apply equally to both men and women.

Observation 2

Age _does not_ appear to have a significant impact on spiritual growth. Responses from people between the ages of nineteen and sixty, with the exception of some small differences, were very similar. This means the research findings indicate the path to spiritual maturity is not correlated to age.

Observation 3

The pattern of spiritual growth _does not_ differ significantly by church. This means the pattern of beliefs, attitudes and behaviors that mark the spiritual journey is similar from church to church. While at this point we have only surveyed seven congregations, the stability of this pattern is a critical finding, which we'll unpack more as we review the six discoveries below.

> *The pattern of beliefs, attitudes and behaviors that mark the spiritual journey is similar from church to church.*

WHAT WE DID FIND:
SIX DISCOVERIES

We made six key discoveries based on the data, starting with one that really caught us off guard.

1. Involvement in church activities does not predict or drive long-term spiritual growth. But there is a "spiritual continuum" that is very predictive and powerful.

We arrived at the conclusion that church activities alone do not drive spiritual growth because we were looking for a framework that would predict increasing levels of agreement with statements like these:

I love God more than anything.

I seek God's guidance for every area of my life.

I have tremendous love for people I know and those I don't know.

We expected to find a direct linear relationship.

When we compared high and low levels of participation in church activities with these statements and related spiritual behaviors (such as evangelism and serving), we expected to find a direct linear relationship. In other words, if increasing church involvement were directly linked to increasing spiritual growth, we would have a chart that looks like this:

This Is What We Would See If Church Activity Drives Spiritual Growth

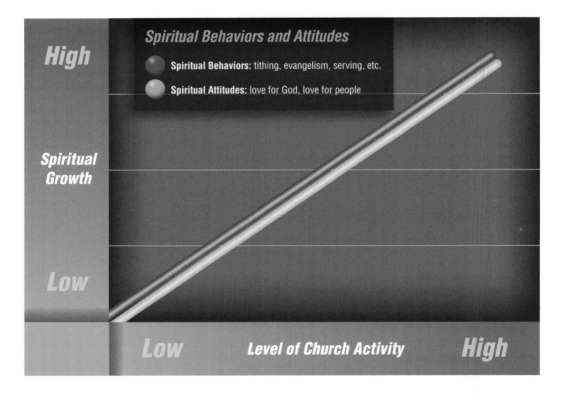

Chart 3-1: If increasing participation in church activities (such as attendance at services and participation in small groups) drives spiritual growth, we would see a direct linear correlation (shown above) between low-medium-high levels of participation and low-medium-high levels of spiritual growth.

Instead our chart looked like this:

Based on Research Results, the Connection Between Church Activity and Spiritual Growth Appears to Be Limited

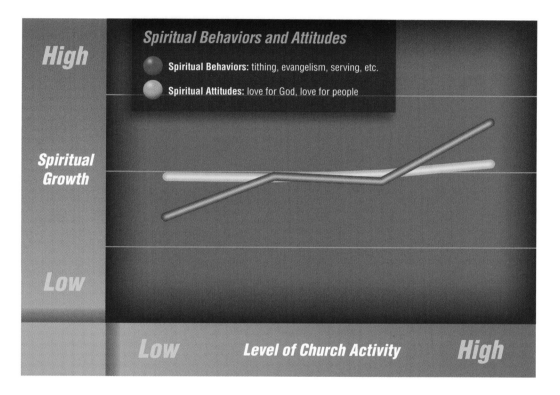

Chart 3-2: The research showed some increase in spiritual behaviors as participation in church activities increases, but very little correlation between low-medium-high levels of participation and increasing "love for God, love for people."

We discovered that higher levels of church activity *did not* predict increasing love for God or increasing love for other people. Now don't misread this! This does not mean that people highly involved in church activities don't love God. It simply means they did not express a greater love for God than people who were less involved in church activities. In other words, an increasing level of activities did not *predict* an increasing love for God.

We found that church involvement drives Christian behavior somewhat, which means that the more people participate in church activities, the more likely they are to serve, tithe, etc. But higher levels of activity do not seem to drive spiritual growth, when defined as "increasing love for God and others."

Church activity alone made no direct impact on growing the heart, as measured by our three statements. It was a flat line—and a stunning discovery for us.

However, when we asked people (in many different ways) how they would describe their spiritual lives, we found what we call a "spiritual continuum" that was highly predictive of spiritual growth (see chart 3-3). In fact, our research experts told us this was one of the *most highly predictive* models they had seen. This means that all the behaviors, attitudes and beliefs we measured related to a growing love for God and others (e.g., spiritual growth) advanced in lockstep with this spiritual continuum. And this continuum centers not on church activities, but rather on a growing relationship with Jesus Christ.

Everything—from daily prayer to Bible reading, to serving and evangelism, and most importantly, love for God and others—moved sharply higher when we looked through the lens of a relationship with Christ (see chart 3-4 on page 37 and "A Closer Look at the Four Segments on the Spiritual Continuum" on pages 38–39).

Everything moved higher when we looked through the lens of a relationship with Christ.

A Spiritual Continuum Emerged from the Research

Exploring Christianity

"I believe in God, but I'm not sure about Christ. My faith is not a significant part of my life."

Growing in Christ

"I believe in Jesus, and I'm working on what it means to get to know him."

Close to Christ

"I feel really close to Christ and depend on him daily for guidance."

Christ-Centered

"God is all I need in my life. He is enough. Everything I do is a reflection of Christ."

Chart 3-3: This framework emerged as the most powerful *predictive* description of how people grow spiritually.

The Spiritual Continuum Predicts Spiritual Growth

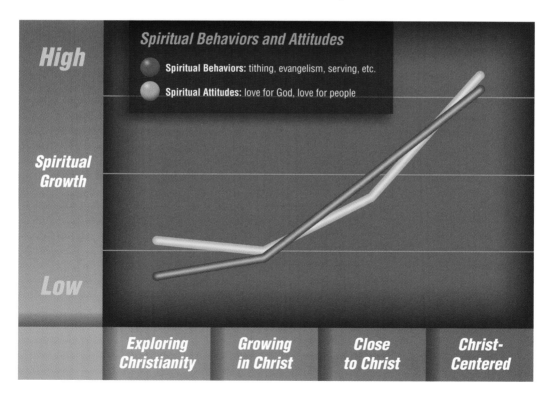

Chart 3-4: The movement of the two lines above shows high correlation between the low-medium-high levels of spiritual growth (spiritual behaviors and spiritual attitudes) and the four segments of the spiritual continuum.

A Closer Look at the Four Segments on

the Spiritual Continuum

Exploring Christianity

"I believe in God, but I'm not sure about Christ. My faith is not a significant part of my life."

Growing in Christ

"I believe in Jesus, and I'm working on what it means to get to know him."

Close to Christ

"I feel really close to Christ and depend on him daily for guidance."

Christ-Centered

"God is all I need in my life. He is enough. Everything I do is a reflection of Christ."

Exploring Christianity

These people are taking the first steps in spiritual growth and are marked by significantly lower levels of agreement with belief statements such as "I believe salvation comes only through Jesus Christ."

Attitudes / Behaviors

- They do not involve God in their daily lives.
- They view the Bible as irrelevant.
- They need others to help them interpret spiritual issues.
- They seek God's guidance only in times of need.
- They do not serve in the church.

Needs

- Seeker services
- Opportunities to connect with others

All the people that fall in any one segment will exhibit essentially the same behaviors, activities and attitudes.

This finding is enormously important. The fact that this continuum is highly predictive means that we can bank on all the people that fall in any one segment to exhibit essentially the same level of spiritual behaviors, activities and attitudes. More importantly, it means that *if* we know the triggers that move people from one segment to another, we could make much better-informed decisions about what ministry initiatives would be most effective in helping them advance along the continuum—for both their individual growth and for overall kingdom impact.

2. Spiritual growth is all about increasing relational closeness to Christ.

We began our search for these triggers—or what Eric Arnson calls the "drivers and barriers"—of spiritual growth by observing that all four segments are defined by the distance or closeness of their relationship to Christ. This second discovery—that spiritual growth is all about increasing relational closeness to Christ—brought great focus

Growing in Christ

These early believers are growing in their faith through church experiences and are also starting to incorporate personal spiritual practices into their normal routine outside of church.

Attitudes/Behaviors

- They are discovering faith.
- They need others to help them interpret spiritual issues.
- They willingly participate in small groups.
- Some of them serve in the church.
- They sometimes read the Bible or Christian books.

Needs

- Small group opportunities
- Basic personal spiritual practices

Close to Christ

These believers report much higher levels of personal spiritual practices than earlier segments. Serving emerges as an important expression of their faith. While their devotion to Christ is growing, they still hold back from full commitment.

Attitudes/Behaviors

- The Bible provides direction for their lives.
- Prayer is central to their lives.
- They have not surrendered everything to Christ.
- Small groups are less important to them.
- Spiritual friends increase in importance to them.
- They serve regularly.

Needs

- Serving opportunities
- Advanced personal spiritual practices

Christ-Centered

These people have fully surrendered their lives to Christ, demonstrated by their dramatically higher levels of spiritual behaviors and attitudes across the board. They "very strongly agree" that they seek God's guidance in every area of their lives—at two times the level of any other segment.

Attitudes/Behaviors

- They love God more than anything.
- For them, prayer is constant conversation with God.
- They help to mentor others.
- Service to others is a way of life.

Needs

- Mentoring opportunities
- Wide range of serving opportunities

to our analytic work. (See "How We Discovered the Spiritual Growth Segments" on page 40 for a more in-depth explanation about the work behind the spiritual continuum.)

But it also created a dilemma. Our first conclusion was that church activities do not predict or drive long-term spiritual growth. However, when you consider the first conclusion in light of this second conclusion, there's potential for some confusion—and soul-searching. If the activities of the church are all about turning people toward Christ and encouraging them to grow spiritually, why doesn't there appear to be a solid connection between participation in church activities and spiritual growth?

Why is there this disconnect? The quick answer: Because God "wired" us first and foremost to be in a growing relationship with him—not with the church. Nature offers us a great illustration of this "wiring" idea in action in the form of migrating birds. Those feathered creatures are somehow equipped with an internal clock and compass that tell them when to take flight and where to go. It's truly awe-inspiring.

How We Discovered the (Spiritual Growth) Segments

Cally Parkinson

THE FOUR SEGMENTS on the spiritual continuum—Exploring, Growing, Close to Christ, and Christ-Centered—are based on a person's *self-reported* relationship with Jesus Christ. Self-reporting might raise questions for some about the validity of the findings. What if people misrepresent where they're really at? Would it skew the results? To address this concern, I'd like to describe how we discovered the segments on the continuum, and also why we believe the data behind the segments is reliable.

We discovered these segments by looking at the data in a number of ways, searching for the best framework to shed light on how people grow spiritually. We analyzed church activities, spiritual behaviors, demographics, life stages and more.

In the end, nothing was more *predictive* of a person's spiritual growth—love of God and love for others—than his or her personal relationship with Jesus Christ. This means that virtually all of our 2.6 million points of data lined up as a direct reflection of how people expressed their relationship with Christ, as reflected on the spiritual continuum.

So the people in the Exploring segment were the *least likely* to serve, tithe, evangelize, pray, read the Bible, declare love for God and belief in Christ. Conversely, the Christ-Centered segment was the *most likely* to demonstrate these behaviors and attitudes. When the research experts say this is one of the most predictive models they've ever seen, this is what they're talking about—that the people in each spiritual growth segment reported behaviors and attitudes that were highly consistent.

You might ask, "What if someone who is far from God, or early in the faith journey, decides to represent themselves more favorably by answering the survey as though they are Christ-Centered?" In other words, if people are deceived about the true state of their spiritual lives, or if they want to skirt the truth, how reliable is the data?

There's nothing to stop that from happening, but it's actually tough to do. It's something like a student who cheats on a multiple-choice quiz. It might work for one quiz, but it's hard to pull off on a comprehensive essay exam or for a full semester of work. Based on a body of work over time—quizzes, class interaction, written reports and other exams—the instructor is likely to have a pretty good handle on the student's true grasp of the subject.

Similarly, according to the experts, a study like this will register less than 5 percent "false" responses—which means less than 5 percent of the people will report attitudes and behaviors that don't align with their self-reported segment on the continuum. Particularly in a category as emotionally charged as spiritual growth, it's unlikely that someone misrepresenting their spiritual classification could maintain a consistent response pattern about their attitudes and behaviors across multiple questions. We did see some evidence of this type of inconsistency in our data, but because its impact is so minimal, it doesn't compromise the overall integrity of the findings.

That's why we have confidence in the reliability of the spiritual continuum—because we see both a powerful, predictive pattern of behaviors and attitudes across all the segments, and because we see a remarkable consistency in the responses. ✦

If God did such an incredible job installing internal homing devices into the wiring of geese and sparrows, imagine the spiritual homing device he wired into the human heart. That's what's so amazing about this research—it sheds the bright light of science on the biblical truth that we are wired to seek God. We are driven to fill the God-shaped holes in our hearts; as Ecclesiastes 3:11 (NLT) tells us, "He has planted eternity in the human heart." There is a passionate instinct born in all of us that desires to draw closer to God. As we draw closer, we begin to see a dramatic change in how we live our lives and relate to other people.

There is a passionate instinct born in all of us that desires to draw closer to God.

The research suggests this instinct is nurtured by two external elements. The first element is the church (we'll talk about the second element a little later), but how the church's role plays out in the spiritual continuum may surprise you.

3. The church is most important in the early stages of spiritual growth. Its role then shifts from being the primary influence to a secondary influence.

The church's role is to help nurture an ongoing (and an "on-growing") relationship with Christ. According to the research, the role of the church changes as people move along the spiritual continuum. Chart 3-5 shows how the role of the church shifts from segment to segment.

The Church's Role as the Primary Influence on Spiritual Growth Becomes Secondary as People Advance Along the Spiritual Continuum

Exploring Christianity

- Weekend services are critical.
- Early connection opportunities are key.

Growing in Christ

- Weekend services remain important.
- Small groups rise in significance.

Close to Christ

- Weekend services decline in importance.
- Small groups drop in importance.
- Serving gains ground.

Christ-Centered

- Church's primary role is to provide serving opportunities.
- Serving the poor is significant.

Chart 3-5: We discovered that as someone moves along the spiritual continuum, the church's role in advancing spiritual growth shifts from providing organized teaching and connection opportunities to providing serving opportunities.

Chart 3-5 illustrates some of the factors that led to our first discovery that the church does not drive long-term spiritual growth. The church is extremely important in the early stages for the Exploring and Growing segments, but its main activities—like weekend services and small groups—decline in importance as people advance along the continuum. The church becomes less of a place to go for spiritual development and to find spiritual relationships, and more of a platform that provides serving opportunities. So its initial strong, central role in spiritual growth seems to shift to something more secondary as people advance to the more Christ-focused spiritual segments.

So if the church isn't the driving force behind the later stages of spiritual growth, what is? That's where the second external element of spiritual growth comes into play: personal spiritual practices. These practices include prayer, journaling, solitude, studying Scripture—things that individuals do on their own to grow in their relationship with Christ. While personal spiritual practices are crucial at all stages of spiritual growth, chart 3-6 demonstrates that they become most important for those who are more spiritually mature.

Personal spiritual practices become most important for those who are more spiritually mature.

Personal Spiritual Practices
Significantly Influence Spiritual Growth

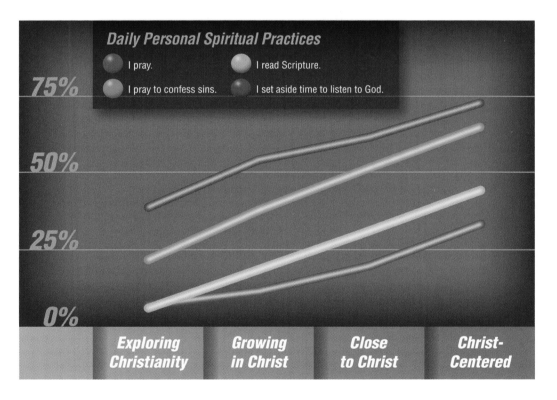

Daily Personal Spiritual Practices
- I pray.
- I pray to confess sins.
- I read Scripture.
- I set aside time to listen to God.

75%

50%

25%

0%

| Exploring Christianity | Growing in Christ | Close to Christ | Christ-Centered |

Chart 3-6: These examples demonstrate the increasing role daily spiritual practices play in people's lives as they grow spiritually.

4. Personal spiritual practices are the building blocks for a Christ-centered life.

This fourth discovery brought with it a pair of key observations:

Spiritual growth is all about growing a relationship with God.

Observation 1

The human spirit is wired by God to search for him, just like birds are wired to fly south for the winter. This deep, internal desire to fill a spiritual void in our souls fuels the momentum behind the spiritual continuum. People want to find God. This natural spiritual wiring propels us along a spiritual growth path that is enriched by influences beyond the church when we enter the more advanced stages of spiritual development.

Observation 2

The research strongly suggests that the church declines in influence as people grow spiritually. Could this mean that the church is dropping the ball on the spiritual growth needs of the most advanced segments? Do people who are developing a more intimate relationship with Christ reach for personal spiritual practices because of the church's ineffectiveness at these later stages? Not necessarily.

Spiritual growth is all about growing a relationship with God through a commitment to, and a deepening relationship with, Jesus Christ. Growing a relationship—any relationship—requires time and energy.

Think about marriage. Great marriages are not built on the first rush of romantic love but on effort, attention and listening. Couples with strong marriages work at them. Similarly, the most devoted Christ-followers spend markedly higher amounts of time dedicated to working on their relationship with Christ by engaging in personal spiritual practices such as prayer, Bible reading and solitude.

> ## Our Conclusion
>
> **Our conclusion based on the data is this: The church doesn't need to handhold people who are moving along in the later stages of the spiritual continuum.** An authentic Christ-Centered life is fundamentally the result of a strong commitment to a growing *personal relationship* with Jesus Christ.

But the research findings are also extremely clear that the church should do everything it can to increase the number of those who are fully surrendered followers of Jesus Christ because, as you'll see in our next discovery, the potential for kingdom impact is huge.

5. A church's most active evangelists, volunteers and donors come from the most spiritually advanced segments.

The evidence is consistent and compelling: the more one grows, the more one serves, tithes and evangelizes. There is absolutely no question about this, according to the research. We see dramatically higher levels of evangelistic activity, volunteering and financial commitment to the church in the Close to Christ and Christ-Centered segments. This is one of the most significant findings we discovered (see chart 3-7 on page 46).

These results caused us to reevaluate deeply rooted beliefs.

This came as a surprise to us. At Willow, we had long operated under the assumption that evangelism fervor is at its highest early on in a person's faith journey. This was based on the thinking that newer believers had more passion for their faith, as well as long-standing relationships with others who had not yet given their lives to Christ. Also, serving is often seen as an early door-opener in the faith journey. These results caused us to reevaluate deeply rooted beliefs.

Percentages specify the percentage of those from each segment who responded as indicated. For example, approximately 50 percent of all those in the Christ-Centered segment responded that they tithe.

Tithing, Serving and Evangelism Advance
Along the Spiritual Continuum

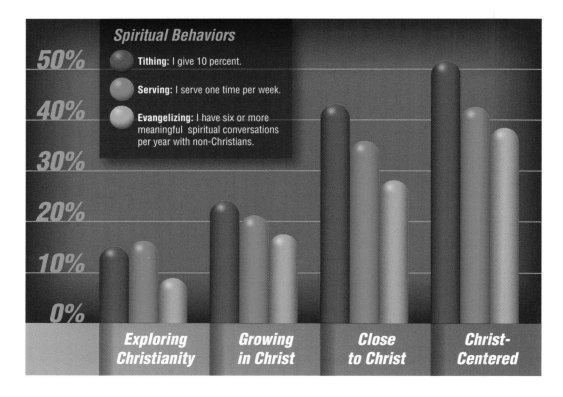

Chart 3-7: As people grow spiritually, they demonstrate increasing faith through their actions. The farther along they are on the spiritual continuum, the more they express their faith to others and donate time and resources to the church.

But our sixth and final discovery was the finding that truly took our breath away. This discovery gives great insight into something we can all empathize with—and something many of us have experienced personally.

We know the path to becoming Christ-Centered is not an easy one. Consider the marriage metaphor again—there are way too many marriages that don't make it. They fail for many reasons, even when people work hard to keep them together. Unfortunately, the path of spiritual growth also has its hazards and potholes. Sometimes life can become overwhelming, and our relationship with Christ hits rocky ground. We knew this was happening in the lives of our congregation, but we were unprepared for its level of impact on our church.

6. More than 25 percent of those surveyed described themselves as spiritually "stalled" or "dissatisfied" with the role of the church in their spiritual growth.

We met two groups of people who acknowledged having spiritual struggles: those who were stalled and those who were dissatisfied. Chart 3-8 shows where they fall on the spiritual continuum.

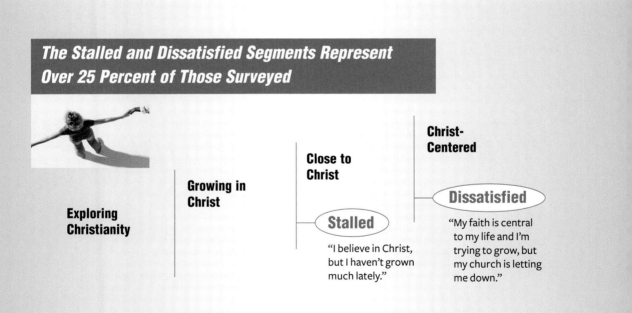

The Stalled and Dissatisfied Segments Represent Over 25 Percent of Those Surveyed

Christ-Centered

Close to Christ

Growing in Christ

Dissatisfied

Exploring Christianity

Stalled

"I believe in Christ, but I haven't grown much lately."

"My faith is central to my life and I'm trying to grow, but my church is letting me down."

Chart 3-8: We discovered two segments that express spiritual struggles. The Stalled segment wrestles with lost momentum in spiritual growth. The Dissatisfied segment demonstrates all the signs of full devotion, but is unhappy with the church.

The Stalled Segment

Those in the first group said, "I believe in Christ, but *I have stalled* and haven't grown much lately." The Stalled segment emerges in the early to middle growing stages of the spiritual continuum. They seem to be holding back or are somehow blocked from spiritual growth and progress. One explanation may be that their personal spiritual practices are significantly off track (see chart 3-9).

Percentages specify the percentage of those from each segment who responded as indicated. For example, approximately 75 percent of all those in the Christ-Centered segment responded that they pray every day.

The Stalled Segment Reports Much Lower Levels of Personal Spiritual Practices Than Other Believer Segments

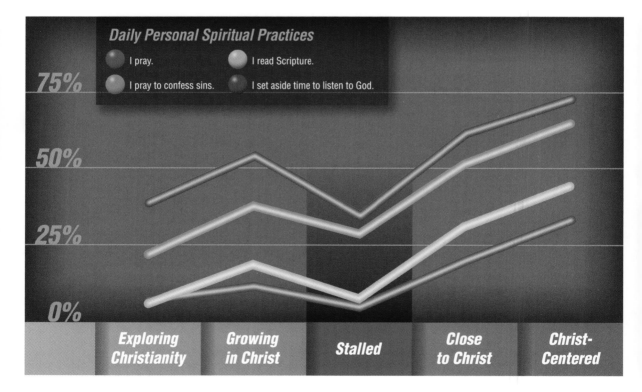

Chart 3-9: The Stalled segment expresses strong spiritual beliefs but is much less likely to engage in daily prayer, Bible study and solitude than the other believer segments (Growing in Christ, Close to Christ and Christ-Centered).

A Closer Look at the (Stalled Segment)

THIS IS AN IMPORTANT segment to understand for two reasons. First, it represents 16 percent of those surveyed, or one out of every six respondents. Second, based on the data outlined below, this segment has issues the church could address. So there's a good chance we can help them get back on a spiritual growth path. Here are some of the things we discovered about those who describe themselves as spiritually stalled.

- They come from the early-to-middle stages of spiritual growth.

- They believe in God and that Jesus is the only road to salvation, but they don't demonstrate that belief through personal spiritual practices. For example, only 7 percent report "setting aside time to read the Bible daily" versus 26 percent of the total sample.

- While 40 percent are very satisfied with the church's role in their spiritual growth, 28 percent are dissatisfied.

- 25 percent—one out of four—are considering leaving the church.

- They acknowledge "significant barriers to spiritual growth" at much higher levels than the other segments. For example:

Addictions (out-of-control spending, gambling, alcohol, pornography, overeating, etc.): 27 percent (50 percent higher than the total sample)

Inappropriate relationships (an emotional or physical affair, other relationships that pull them away from God): 16 percent (more than 60 percent higher than the total sample)

Emotional issues (depression, anger, stuffing emotions, etc.): 48 percent (35 percent higher than the total sample)

Not prioritizing one's spiritual life (spending more time on other things like TV, Internet, e-mails, movies, shopping): 89 percent (19 percent higher than the total sample)

Our Observation: The Stalled segment seems to include people at the beginning of the faith journey who have run into difficult life circumstances or come face-to-face with a personal weakness that is incompatible with following Christ. Because their Christian walk is not deeply rooted in spiritual practices (daily prayer and Bible study, etc.), they feel rudderless—and consequently dissatisfied with their spiritual life. Less than 1 percent are extremely/very satisfied (versus 15 percent of the total sample) with their spiritual lives. And, as noted above, 25 percent are considering leaving the church. ✦

However, the Stalled segment is far more complex than this simple explanation. They are almost bipolar in their church satisfaction ratings: some are very satisfied, but a high percentage is dissatisfied, and a quarter of them say they are considering leaving the church. They also report higher levels of personal issues, like addictions, that are "significant barriers" to their spiritual growth. (For more information, see "A Closer Look at the Stalled Segment" on page 49.) This segment will be the subject of much more attention and scrutiny as we develop our research database with additional churches in the future.

The Dissatisfied Segment

The second group is the Dissatisfied segment. This group will also get much more attention in future research, because it is an incredibly important segment to understand.

These people are active evangelists, volunteers and donors in the church.

Whereas those in the Stalled segment tend to come out of the early to middle stages of faith, the Dissatisfied segment—the people who are most unhappy with their church—tend to come from the segments that are more Christ-focused. These people are active evangelists, volunteers and donors in the church. Take a look at chart 3-10.

The Dissatisfied segment is similar to the Close to Christ segment in many aspects—not only in the spiritual behaviors, but also in their commitment to daily personal spiritual practices, such as prayer, Bible study, etc. This is a key differentiator between the Dissatisfied and the Stalled segments.

Thus, the Dissatisfied segment has people who are some of the most involved in the church and who are trying to grow in their faith. However, the research shows they are also the ones most likely to report that they are considering leaving the church.

The Dissatisfied Segment Reports Levels of Tithing, Serving and Evangelism Comparable to the Most Advanced Segments

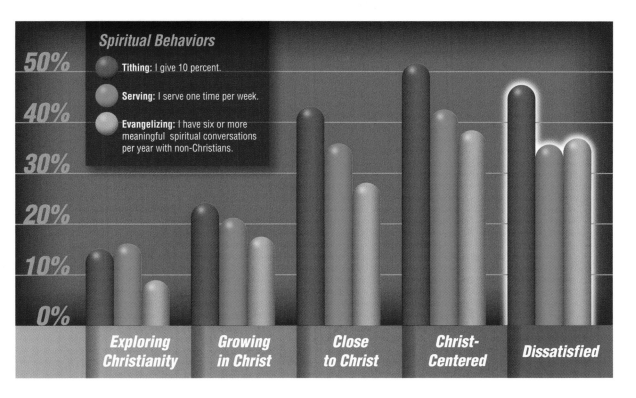

Spiritual Behaviors

- **Tithing:** I give 10 percent.
- **Serving:** I serve one time per week.
- **Evangelizing:** I have six or more meaningful spiritual conversations per year with non-Christians.

Segments: Exploring Christianity · Growing in Christ · Close to Christ · Christ-Centered · Dissatisfied

Chart 3-10: The Dissatisfied segment demonstrates faith through their actions. Only the Christ-Centered segment reports higher levels of tithing and evangelism.

When researcher Eric Arnson saw these numbers, he was stunned. Using the marketplace as a reference, he explained that typically, the more engaged someone becomes in a product category, the higher their level of loyalty is to their favorite brand. In other words, if I drink a lot of soft drinks and my favorite is Diet Coke, my loyalty and likelihood to recommend Diet Coke to other people is extremely high.

In our case, that would mean that a rising level of satisfaction with the church should go hand-in-hand with increasing spiritual growth. Yet we found that wasn't necessarily true. Generally speaking, the higher the level of engagement—the higher the level of commitment to Christ—the more likely it is that satisfaction with the church will be lukewarm.

The higher the level of engagement, the more likely it is that satisfaction with the church will be lukewarm.

The number of dissatisfied people is not inconsequential. On average, in the seven churches we've reviewed, it's about 10 percent of a congregation. So one out of every ten people in the church is unhappy—and often extremely unhappy. Take a look at chart 3-11.

Percentages specify the percentage of those from each segment who responded as indicated. For example, 26 percent of all those in the Dissatisfied segment strongly agreed that their church "provides compelling worship services."

The Dissatisfied Segment's Unhappiness with the Church Is Pronounced

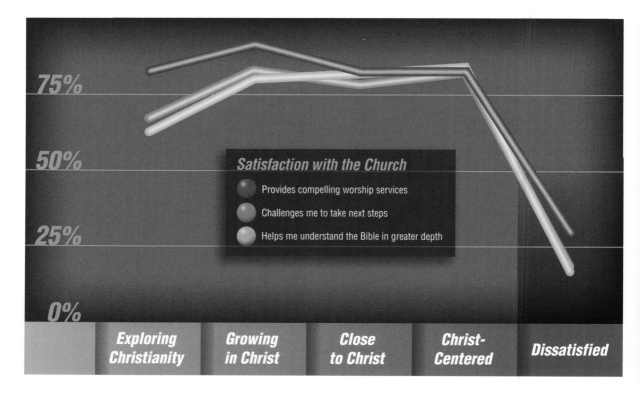

Chart 3-11: We measured thirty-two church benefits in addition to the three noted above. Across the board, the Dissatisfied segment marked "strongly agree" much less often (approximately one-third as often) as the other segments.

What's with these dissatisfied people? There is no easy answer to this—at least, not yet! But it is certainly true that their level of expectation for what the church can and should deliver is much higher than any other segment. (For more information, see "A Closer Look at the Dissatisfied Segment" on page 53.)

Cally Parkinson | # A Closer Look at the (Dissatisfied) Segment

IT IS CRITICAL to understand the Dissatisfied segment, because all the data indicates they are not simply believers in Christ; they are true Christ-followers. But they are also highly likely to consider leaving their church. Most challenging: they probably represent one-tenth of your congregation. Here are some of the things we discovered about those who describe themselves as dissatisfied.

The Dissatisfied segment includes people from the more advanced spiritual growth segments, so they exhibit all the signs of full devotion:

They regularly attend weekend services:
- 96 percent attend three to four times a month (same as total sample). They desire much more challenge and depth from the services.
- 20 percent rate services as "outstanding" or "excellent" (versus 71 percent of the total sample).
- 60 percent would like to see "more in-depth Bible teaching" (versus 30 percent of the total), and 56 percent want more challenge (versus 19 percent of the total).

They participate in small groups (55 percent meet once a month or more).

They volunteer at church (61 percent once a month or more).

They serve those in need (25 percent at least quarterly).

They tithe (31 percent).

They're diligent in their personal efforts to grow their faith through daily Bible study/ reflection (39 percent versus 26 percent of the total sample) and daily prayer (59 percent versus 56 percent of the total).

Nevertheless, 63 percent are considering leaving the church due to much lower levels of satisfaction with the church across the board. Whether the topic is church services, Bible classes or small groups, their satisfaction responses are significantly lower than those of the total sample.

Our Observation: To dig into what's really going on with this segment, we combed through thirty-five statements and satisfaction ratings about church benefits, and we found something interesting. The two statements rated lowest by the Dissatisfied segment were:

- *"The church keeps me on track as I try to lead a Christian life."* Just 7 percent reported being satisfied versus 47 percent for the total, a multiple difference of almost seven times.

- *"The church helps me find a spiritual mentor."* Just 4 percent reported being satisfied versus 25 percent for the total, a multiple difference of more than six times.

Although the Dissatisfied segment appears totally aligned with the attitudes and behaviors related to a Christ-Centered life, they still want the church to help "keep them on track," to hold them accountable and keep them challenged. A tool like a personal spiritual growth plan might address some of those needs. But they also seem to want a personal growth coach or spiritual mentor. That may be what would truly "keep them on track" and from walking out the back door. ✦

So even though the Dissatisfied segment tends to be more actively involved with personal spiritual practices than the Stalled segment, data indicates that both the Dissatisfied and Stalled segments still look almost exclusively to the church to lead their spiritual growth.

Neither segment seems to realize that much of the responsibility for their spiritual growth belongs to them.

Both segments tend to voice complaints about the need for more in-depth teaching, more connection opportunities, more serving options and more of about everything else they feel is missing from their church experience. But at the heart of their unhappiness may be the fact that neither segment seems to realize that much of the responsibility for their spiritual growth belongs to *them*. This is the big "aha."

And it begs the question: Who should have pointed this out to them? Who should have helped them to begin taking more responsibility for their own spiritual growth? The answer is pretty obvious.

THE ROLE AND OPPORTUNITY FOR THE CHURCH

Based on the research, the church seems to make its biggest impact at the start of the spiritual continuum—when people are beginning to explore Christianity and are in the early growing stages of faith. Similarly, parents are most influential to their children in the early years. As they grow toward adolescence, children sprout wings of maturity and then leave the family nest for their own life path.

But even as children strike out on their own, parents remain influential. My children are ages twenty and twenty-five. By most definitions, they are adults. But in recent weeks I've helped one of them navigate the emotions of a romantic breakup, and the other one plan a wedding. I'm still important and influential in their lives, but in a different way than when I was changing their diapers or helping with homework.

The decline of the church's influence as people mature spiritually suggests that the church may have put too much emphasis on the spiritual equivalent of the diaper-changing and homework-helping stage of care. Much like parents, the church may need to shift its relationship with its maturing disciples into something different in order to maintain an appropriate level of influence and provide the support they need.

As people work to grow in their personal relationship with Christ—a relationship that presumably has benefited from a foundation of solid theology and encouragement from church teaching—the institution of the church becomes less central to their faith development. This is as it should be—just as parents need to celebrate a child's increasing independence.

But the church also has to be honest when it considers the question: Could we be better parents? The research suggests that the answer is yes. Our analysis paints the picture of the church being too preoccupied with the early growing years, leaving the spiritual adolescents to find their own way—without preparing them for the journey.

Imagine the kingdom gains if the church figured out the ideal way to parent or coach Christ-followers all along the spiritual continuum. Imagine the impact if all those Stalled and Dissatisfied people were put back on track and moved into higher stages of spiritual maturity and productivity. Imagine what would happen if the church could create pathways that urge those who are Growing and Close to Christ to begin leading truly Christ-Centered lives.

Imagine the kingdom gains if the church figured out the ideal way to parent or coach Christ-followers all along the spiritual continuum.

If the church could recast its role to take advantage of even a small portion of the opportunities suggested in this work and illustrated in the chart below, the kingdom gains could be extraordinary. So the stakes are incredibly high. But the strategy for success may be incredibly simple—as simple as becoming better spiritual "parents" for our people.

The Church's Greatest Opportunity Is to Increase Its Influence with the Most Devoted Christ-Followers

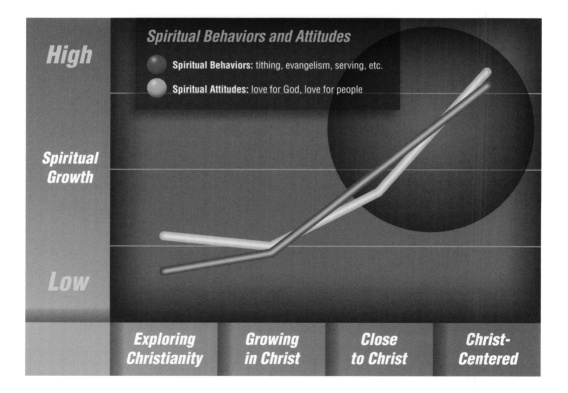

Chart 3-12: The data suggests that the church provides minimal support for those who are most devoted to Christ. Since these people are the best equipped and most motivated advocates for Christ, providing them with increased coaching and encouragement could reap great gains for the kingdom.

RECAP OF FINDINGS COMPARED TO WHERE WE STARTED

In the world of data and research, it's always a good idea to take a step back and revisit the assumptions you had going into your research. If you don't, it's easy to end up on analytical rabbit trails that may be interesting, but not really significant to your biggest issues and concerns.

Since we started our work three years ago, we've tried to keep an eye on our original three hypotheses. Here's how our findings to date compare with those initial assumptions.

It's always a good idea to take a step back and revisit the assumptions you had.

Our Hypotheses Compared to Our Discoveries

Our Hypotheses	What We Discovered
There is a migration path for spiritual growth based on church activities.	A spiritual migration path exists, but it is not defined by a person's church involvement. Instead, it is defined by a person's relationship with Jesus Christ.
The most effective evangelism tool is a spiritual conversation.	Spiritual conversations are important to evangelism, but the most effective outreach strategy—bar none—is to motivate the most Christ-Centered people. They are the best evangelists, best volunteers and most generous donors in the church.
Spiritual friendships are a key driver to spiritual growth.	Meeting the need for connection and genuine spiritual relationships is crucial to spiritual growth. Yet organized efforts to create these environments appear to be effective only in the earlier stages of spiritual growth.

We can take a new, fresh look at the role and the potential of the church.

When we look back at the early hypotheses, we have to acknowledge that our vision of what we might discover was pretty limited. We went in with some "blinders" on, believing that church activities were the predominant drivers of spiritual growth, and we just assumed the church would show up as the central force in the spiritual walk of our most Christ-Centered people. We were not prepared to discover that so many people are stalled in their spiritual lives, and certainly not prepared to find that some of our best disciples were among those most dissatisfied with the church. We were also surprised that personal spiritual practices played such a critical role—showing up as the primary catalyst for growth in the most advanced spiritual segments.

Given the large gaps between our original hypotheses and these results—especially the unanticipated findings related to the Stalled and Dissatisfied segments, the role of personal spiritual practices and the overall decline in influence of the church at the most advanced stages of spiritual growth—we can only reach one conclusion. God seems to have used this work to reveal some disturbing truths to us so we can take a new, fresh look at the role and the potential of the church.

And we believe there's a lot more God wants us to learn . . .

THE BEST DISCOVERY OF ALL

One of the most amazing discoveries the data points to is this: We've only scratched the surface. We will continue to collect data from an increasing number of churches and hope that what we discover in the days to come will shed more light on some of the biggest issues facing churches today. We believe we've seen only the tip of the iceberg.

We've only scratched the surface . . .

We've just begun to enrich our findings with data from other churches. As this writing goes to press, we are launching another survey to twenty-five more churches across the United States. The depth and breadth of our database will increase, and so will our ability to evaluate the effectiveness of things like various small group strategies, service formats and a host of other church activities across an even wider range of church models. We hope to be able to understand, in depth and in detail, the impact of things like Internet-based products and services on people's spiritual lives, as well as different approaches to prayer, journaling, solitude and other personal spiritual practices.

*Join us
on this
adventure
of divine
discovery.*

Our vision is that eventually people from hundreds of churches will participate in the survey study, including churches beyond the United States. Our hope is to make this growing wealth of findings and insights available to everyone and anyone who is committed to advancing God's kingdom. That's our plan. That's our dream. And we think it's God's dream too.

We invite you to join us on this adventure of divine discovery that has no roadmap . . . other than the one God has wired into the human heart.

GREG L. HAWKINS

REVE

4 SO WHAT CAN YOU DO NOW?

**THREE NEXT STEPS
YOU CAN TAKE
TODAY**

decisions

AFTER CONSIDERING ALL THE DATA and discoveries, it's fair to ask, "So what?" It's also essential to wrestle with tough questions and begin to take action. Three next-step ideas help leaders and churches who are ready to address the question, "Where are we?"

4

SO WHAT CAN YOU DO NOW?

Legendary college basketball coach John Wooden had a sign in his office at UCLA that stated: "When you're through learning, you're through."

One of the things I've enjoyed most about this research is how much I've learned. I've learned that it's possible to get a glimpse of what's happening in someone's heart as they strive to grow in their love for God and their love for others. It's possible to analyze which areas of ministry help people move along the spiritual continuum toward Christ-Centered lives—and which ministries do not. And I've learned that these patterns are not just unique to Willow but are shared by six other congregations across the United States.

But I didn't set out on this journey just to learn. I wanted to use our learning to create a strategic plan for Willow that would guide our decisions for the years to come. So what happened with that process?

Well, needless to say, the insights from this research really rocked us. I remember the nervous anticipation Cally, Eric and I felt before we walked into Bill Hybels' office to tell him what we'd discovered. How do you tell your boss (and the founding pastor of the church) that the church isn't as effective as we'd thought? To his credit, Bill openly embraced our work and was the driving force in bringing these insights into the forefront of our thinking.

"When you're through learning, you're through."

A NEW
VISION AND STRATEGY

It took us more than two years to assimilate the results from this research and to discern what God wanted us to do about it, but eventually a new vision and a strategy emerged. In April 2007, we unveiled a strategic plan to our congregation that features some new initiatives catalyzed by the research.

We believe God is challenging us to act on what we've learned so far.

We are convinced of one thing as we move forward: we don't know if our plans will work, but we are committed to learning as we go. We might head in a wrong direction, but we would rather make a move than stand still, because we believe God is challenging us to act on what we've learned so far.

Before digging into the steps you can take, I thought it might be helpful to tell you about some of the things that are a part of our new strategic plan. It's important to understand that this is how Willow is acting on the findings; these are *not* recommendations for other churches to follow. Here are three strategic changes we've made as a direct result of what the research revealed.

1. Our Message to the Congregation Has to Change

Historically at Willow, no matter where someone is along the spiritual continuum, our message has been the same: "We know what you need, and we can meet those needs for you." We now know this approach hasn't always served our congregation well. In many cases we have created an unhealthy dependence and inappropriate levels of expectation among those who call Willow home.

One of the first things we did was to tell our congregation that we've been wrong for thinking it was our job to meet all of their spiritual growth needs. When Bill laid out the new strategic plan to the congregation in April 2007, he said, "We have been wrong. We need to rethink the coaching we give you as you pursue your spiritual growth."

That sent a strong signal to the congregation that we heard what they told us in the surveys. We understood we were not helping some of them grow, and we were going to make changes.

We want to move people.

We want to move people from dependence on the church to a growing interdependent partnership with the church. We have to let people know early on in their journey that they need to look beyond the church to grow. Getting a weekly dose or two of what the church has to offer (even if it is great) will never be sufficient spiritual nutrition for survival, let alone growth. Our people need to learn to feed themselves through personal spiritual practices that allow them to deepen their relationship with Christ.

We want to transition the role of the church from spiritual parent to spiritual coach.

2. We Need to Coach Next Steps

When a church is working out of a dependence model, ministry is rather straightforward: Figure out what you think everyone needs and then provide it through a program or an activity. But what might an *interdependent* model look like? What is the role of the church in such a model?

We want to transition the role of the church from spiritual parent to spiritual coach. When you go to a gym to get physically fit, a trainer often assesses your current strengths and weaknesses. Based on that assessment, the trainer prescribes a personalized workout plan. If you are really unfit, or at the beginning of your "physical fitness journey," there are certain things you should do. Then, as you grow stronger and advance in your abilities, you begin to do different things. There is no "one-size-fits-all" fitness plan.

Similarly, there is no one-size-fits-all spiritual growth plan. That's why one of our new initiatives is to create a tool everyone can use to assess the current state of their relationship with Christ ("spiritual fitness"), and then to recommend a customized growth or "workout" plan that provides direction for their next step spiritually. We believe it is essential for us to help everyone answer the question, "What's next for me?" This tool is currently in development, and we hope to present it to the congregation within the coming year.

3. We Need to Extend the Impact of Our Weekend Services

Weekend services are an important element in the spiritual growth of people in the early stages of their spiritual journey, but they have less value for those farther along the spiritual continuum. One of our initiatives is to extend the impact of the weekend service to meet the needs of those who are farther along the journey. We are still brainstorming numerous ideas, but let me share with you one thing we recently tried.

It is essential to help everyone answer the question, "What's next for me?"

During a five-week series on the book of James, we distributed a free journal that was designed to help people take next steps wherever they were along the spiritual continuum. We had pages for taking notes (for the Exploring), as well as questions that an individual could use throughout the week to further reflect on that week's passage of Scripture (for those Growing in Christ). It also had study questions that people could use in their small groups (also for Growing in Christ) or with a spiritual friend (for those Close to Christ) to help process what they were learning. We even included insights from a biblical commentary for those who wanted to dig deeper (for the Christ-Centered).

The response from the congregation was incredibly positive. Afterward, we interviewed people who used the journal, and we discovered it helped people in segments all across the spiritual continuum. In the future, we plan to continue leveraging things we are already doing, like our weekend services, in similar ways.

THREE PRACTICAL NEXT STEPS YOU CAN TAKE

After processing these findings for three years, we are just now starting to make some major ministry changes.

Why the long delay?

Honestly, it took a while for all of this to sink in. We went through our own stages of denial—anger, sadness, depression, the works—until we could finally embrace the brutal truth: we needed to change.

Just as we needed to, I'm guessing you will take some time to get a better understanding of all of this information. But if you are wondering if there is anything you can do now, the answer is yes. And the good news is your first step doesn't have to be in-depth research. We hope our research can get you started.

Here are three steps that can be used as a starting point for your church. Best of all, you can try any of them beginning today.

1. Ask more than "How many?"

2. Go beyond "How are you?"

3. Ask "How does that help someone grow?"

1. Ask More Than "How Many?"

For too long the church has asked the question "How many?" as the standard way of measuring "success" in ministry. How many decisions for Christ? How many baptisms? How many members? How many in small groups? And on it goes.

This is not a bad question to ask. "How many?" helps us see what brings people to our churches and which ministries are of interest to them. "How many?" is a good question—especially when there are follow-up questions.

How many? decisions for Christ? members baptisms? attend each weekend? tithe? are in small groups? actively serve?

A great first step you can take for your church is to make sure "How many?" isn't the only question you ask when measuring the impact of your ministry efforts. In almost any discussion following a service or an event, "How many?" is inevitably the first question asked. However, the next time you hear the "How many?" question, follow it up by asking, "How did this event help people grow?" And if you want to get even deeper, ask, "Which segment of people was this event intended to help, and did it actually help them?"

Senior leaders need to take the initiative to ask the follow-up questions. If you don't, who will? Asking follow-up questions starts a whole new kind of conversation within your church. No longer will "How many?" be the sole driver of what defines success for a service, an event or an activity.

Changing the conversation is a powerful tool in the hands of a leader. There is something about language that is transforming. As it says in Proverbs 16:23: "From a wise mind comes wise speech; the words of the wise are persuasive" (NLT). Changing the conversation by asking more than "How many?" is the beginning of reorienting how you view your church's effectiveness—and how the staff and members of your church view it as well.

Changing the conversation is a powerful tool in the hands of a leader.

2. Go Beyond "How Are You?"

It's one of the beauties of being a ministry leader: you talk with the people in your congregation almost every day. The second step you can take is to continue doing just that—but to add some new questions to the mix as well. Anyone can ask, "How are you?" but what would happen if you went beyond that?

What you hear could change your church and the way you do ministry in a big way.

When you get the opportunity and it's appropriate, ask more probing questions in your one-on-one conversations. Ask about their personal spiritual practices. Ask about their satisfaction with the church's role in their spiritual growth. Ask what your church could do differently to help them grow.

The answers you hear will help you better understand where each person is on the spiritual continuum, and how the church is helping (or not helping) them take the next steps. Make it a point to talk with people from each of the four major segments on the spiritual continuum. Challenge them to tell you the truth—not just what they think you want to hear. But beware. What you hear could change your church and the way you do ministry in a big way.

Here are some questions that could open up healthy dialogues:

- *How is your relationship with God?*

- *What's helping you grow spiritually these days?*

- *What ministry is making a difference in your life? How?*

- *What could the church do differently that would help you grow more?*

Now comes the tough part . . .

What do you do with what you hear? Resist the urge to be defensive if people say things that are hard to hear. Instead, listen intently. Afterward, reflect on what you heard; let it sink in. If you hear the same things over and over again, chances are there's some truth to it.

That means you need to be prepared to act on what you hear. Not reactively to just one person's input, but strategically by planning for changes based on what you hear regularly over time.

3. Ask "How Does That Help Someone Grow?"

To assess the effectiveness of your ministry, ask of each ministry program, "How does that help someone grow?" You won't need a big research project to get started. You won't even need a computer. Just grab a sheet of paper and a pencil to draw your own chart, or use the blank chart included on page 107.

Using the framework outlined below, list in the left column the ministry programs your church offers for adults. You can list just the major ministries or all of them. You should then have something that looks like the chart on the next page.

Listen intently. Reflect on what you hear. Let it sink in.

MINISTRY PROGRAM	EXPLORING CHRISTIANITY	GROWING IN CHRIST	CLOSE TO CHRIST	CHRIST-CENTERED
Worship services				
Small groups				
Recovery ministries				
Women's Bible study				
Men's breakfast				

Now evaluate your ministries based on level of impact you think they have on the spiritual growth of people in each segment. Use the following scale: High Impact, Medium Impact, Low Impact. For example, you might assess the impact of your worship services like this:

MINISTRY PROGRAM	EXPLORING CHRISTIANITY	GROWING IN CHRIST	CLOSE TO CHRIST	CHRIST-CENTERED
Worship services	High	High	High	Medium

Next, ask some of your staff to do their own assessments (without showing them yours). Then compare assessments. That should create some interesting conversations. If you are really brave, ask some of the volunteers who serve in those ministries to do their own assessments. What are their opinions of how well their ministry helps people in different segments grow?

See if you can reach a consensus. Note the gaps. Are the needs of some segments not being met? For example, when we did this at Willow, we discovered that we had no ministry that trained people in personal spiritual disciplines. It's a huge miss we are in the process of addressing.

This is not a precise science, but if you can start thinking like this now, you might discover something that will dramatically affect your ministries.

MOVING AHEAD

We want to try new things and to keep reassessing what helps people grow.

We have a renewed excitement around Willow these days because of the important questions this research forced us to ask, and the answers we are searching for as a result. We sense that the steps we are taking will enable us to help more people grow in their love of God and their love for others. We want to learn, to try new things and to keep reassessing what helps people grow more deeply in their relationship with Christ.

We don't just want to learn from within our own church. We would love to learn from you. After you've finished this book, I invite you to join in the conversation by logging on to our website **www.revealnow.com** and providing us with your feedback and

www.revealnow.com

thoughts—not only about what you've read, but also about how your church helps people move along the spiritual growth continuum. Our hope is that by asking questions and working through them together with other churches, we all will gain a better understanding of how spiritual growth is happening (or not happening) in our churches.

We are not through learning about this topic. In fact, it's safe to say that the learning has just begun.

Three years into this project, I still find myself sometimes lying awake at night thinking about the church. Only now, instead of feeling anxious, I eagerly anticipate our next round of findings and the impact they might have on the church at large.

At the end of the day, we all want to hit the pillow at night knowing we are making the impact God has called us to make. And if someone happens to show up with a million dollars for our church, we'll have a much better understanding of where to invest that gift so that it will have the greatest kingdom impact.

Greg L. Hawkins

AFTERWORD:
WHERE ARE *YOU?*

The Lord our God has secrets known to no one. We are not accountable for
them, but *we and our children are accountable forever for all that he has
revealed to us,* so that we may obey all the terms of these instructions.
Deuteronomy 29:29 (NLT, emphasis added)

When it was time to choose a title, the name REVEAL
seemed right for this book. It also felt like a good fit for the ongoing
research we are doing about how churches can empower their people to move toward Christ-Centered lives. We truly believe that
God revealed new insights to us about the people of our church—
and how our church can help them grow closer to Christ. As the
verse in Deuteronomy says, now that it has been revealed to us, we
are accountable to act upon it.

With research tools that enabled us to measure the unseen, we
went into our 2004 congregational survey with new lenses we
hoped would lead to new discoveries. We hoped we would be able to
dive deeply into the hearts of our people to find out what was working and not working when it came to spiritual growth.

We were able to do that—and so much more.

We believe the findings we have shared with you have truly been
revealed to us. We were blessed with an incredible set of circumstances that brought the right people and the right pieces together,
enabling us to measure spiritual growth in a thoughtful, deliberate,

*We hoped
we would
be able to
dive deeply
into the
hearts of
our people.*

Do what you can now, and then continue to wrestle with the implications.

rigorous and ongoing way. The piles of data and the expert analysis have confirmed the viability of this work and attested to its thoroughness again and again.

What we found has changed the way Willow Creek looks at its role as a church. We have a whole new way of thinking about how we can impact the lives of the people who call Willow home—especially people who are moving farther along the spiritual continuum. However, it's also important to remember that we wrestled with the study findings for nearly three years before we were ready to implement any new strategies based on what we discovered about the church's role in spiritual growth.

So we know that all of this information can be overwhelming. But please, don't throw up your hands and walk away. Instead, let the enormity of what's been revealed to you serve as motivation to take a new look at your church and its ministries. Do what you can now, and then continue to wrestle with the implications as your church moves ahead with new strategies in the months and years to come.

My prayer is that you are encouraged by what you've read, and that you're ready to join us in an ongoing conversation. Through our website **www.revealnow.com**, our desire is to maintain an open conversation with you and other church leaders who are willing to ask more than "How many?"—so we can learn from each other as we learn together.

God put a call on your heart to make a difference in the lives of people he loves—people he desires to grow ever closer to him. I encourage you to ask God to **REVEAL** to you what he wants to do in your church.

Then get ready to answer the question God has been asking from the beginning of time:

"Where are you?"

APPENDICES

Eric Arnson

appendix **1**

THE ART AND SCIENCE OF MEASURING THE UNSEEN

In the early years of the science of marketing strategy development, everything was based on demographics. Huge companies were built by tapping into demographic trends, such as Sears staking out suburbia as the next retail growth frontier following the Depression, and McDonald's capturing the fancy of overscheduled, car-crazy, baby-boomer families.

However, in the last twenty years, the sophistication level of the marketing world has increased enormously. Today, professional market strategists and analysts like me have moved well beyond looking at simple demographics to learn what makes a market tick.

My career has been devoted to building and executing research techniques that help businesses understand the unseen factors that motivate their customers. What I do—with lots of help from expert statisticians, survey designers and analyst colleagues—is look below the surface of demographics to the emotions, motivations and needs that really drive consumer behavior.

In other words, I measure the unseen.

I have always found this fascinating—asking questions about how and why people make emotional commitments to things like products and brands. For example, why is it that your friend will drink any soft drink that's offered, but you'll settle for nothing less than a Diet Coke?

How does The Weather Channel become your trusted expert—not only for weather conditions, but also travel conditions, pollen conditions and anything else related to travel and the outdoors?

What is it about John Deere that encourages such fierce loyalty in customers—not only to Deere equipment, but also to the brand at large?

The business implications of these types of questions are huge. But it's nothing compared to the eternal implications of measuring the spiritually unseen.

KEY DEVELOPMENTS IN THE SCIENCE OF MARKET RESEARCH

Laddering begins with a product attribute, then climbs to functional benefits and ultimately to emotional benefits.

My professional interest in discovering how and why people make purchasing decisions began during my first job at Procter & Gamble. At the time, Procter & Gamble was heavily focused on emphasizing the attributes and functional benefits of their products. Historically, they gained market share because their products outperformed the competition—they created products that were whiter, brighter, moister, etc. And they had the data to prove these claims. Over time, however, competitive brands made improvements to close the gap. (After all, a cake can only be so moist before it becomes pudding!)

Along the way, Bill Hahn, a consumer scientist for the company, pioneered several consumer-based research approaches, including a highly effective technique called laddering. In laddering, one begins with a product attribute, then climbs the ladder to get to the functional benefits and ultimately to the emotional benefits. Starbucks is a well-known contemporary brand that we can use to illustrate this point (see "Starbucks: A Case Study" on page 81).

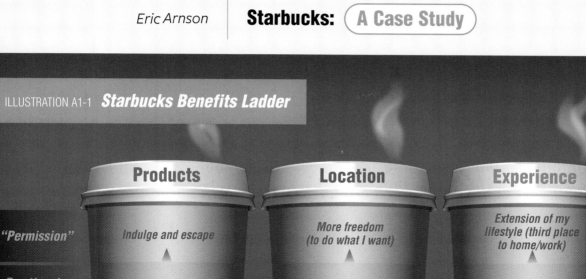

ILLUSTRATION A1-1 *Starbucks Benefits Ladder*

	Products	Location	Experience
"Permission"	Indulge and escape ▲	More freedom (to do what I want) ▲	Extension of my lifestyle (third place to home/work) ▲
Emotional Platform	Makes me feel important ▲	In control of my time ▲	Empowers me ▲
Functional Platform	Order customized just for me ▲	Accessible, efficient ▲	Comfortable, productive ▲
Functional Benefits	Experienced and friendly baristas ▲	Convenient to home and work ▲	Space to work and socialize ▲
Product Features	Premier drinks, indulgent treats and snacks	Extended hours, fast service, many locations	Comfortable seats, wireless Internet, music

SOURCE: Mark Mitten and Eric Arnson (Originate Consulting)

ACROSS THE BOTTOM RUNG of the ladder, you see the product attributes or features that are key to Starbucks' offering—premier coffee drinks, fast service, many locations, wireless Internet, etc. The ladder builds by adding the functional benefits, then the emotional benefits associated with the product's features. For example, Starbucks' many locations, extended hours and fast service (in the "location" ladder bar) provide functional benefits of convenience and accessibility. Those functional benefits allow people to feel more "in control of" their time—an emotional benefit.

The concept at the top of the ladders—"permission"—is extremely important because this is where expansion of products and services is likely to be welcomed by targeted customers. So Starbucks' expansion into breakfast sandwich products is a logical extension of their brand benefits and directly associated with their primary product, coffee. It also shows they understand their customers. ✦

Emotional benefits build stronger brand loyalty than just functional benefits.

Bill Hahn helped demonstrate—both qualitatively and quantitatively—that emotional benefits could build stronger brand loyalty than just the functional benefits that the company had been relying on. He parlayed that learning into concept development, enabling the company to create new products with specific emotional benefits in mind, just like the Starbucks example.

Later, when Bill and I worked together in the cosmetics industry, he expanded the concept of emotional benefits to the broader idea of intangible benefits. That's because he discovered that motivations and attitudes—in addition to emotions—were also key components of brand loyalty. This expanded our thinking beyond how a product or service made you "feel" (emotions), to what spurred you to try the product in the first place (motivations) and whether or not there is a particular mindset that influenced your actions (attitudes).

This type of work ideally raises an even bigger issue: not just how a customer feels about the product or service they are currently getting, but what the *unmet* needs are that offer new and potentially better opportunities. In other words, am I offering the right product or service? See "The Weather Channel: A Case Study" on page 83 for a demonstration of how this works.

The Weather Channel: A Case Study

Eric Arnson

WHEN THE WEATHER CHANNEL was getting started in 1982, they went after a segment of the television audience they affectionately called "weather enthusiasts"—people who were into weather phenomena, almost like amateur meteorologists. My company came in and said, "Why don't we ask a broader question: How does weather impact someone's life?"

We found a number of ways weather impacts daily life, including:

- Commuting—both on the roads and in the air
- Outdoor activities—working, gardening, sports and leisure
- Major weather conditions—disruptions caused by harsh conditions

Our research showed that customers wanted to plan ahead—to understand how the weather would affect their daily life. To some, it was a question of, "Should I bring an umbrella?" For others, it meant setting the alarm thirty minutes earlier because the commute was going to be a long one. Or worse, it was wondering, "Do I have to spend another day on the road because my flights are delayed or canceled?" The Weather Channel was all about planning: making the unpredictable—weather—predictable.

Through this consumer lens, The Weather Channel became much more than a source for information about weather conditions. It was also a source for travel conditions. That's why today they show a traffic report every ten minutes, because if someone is planning to get from point A to point B, they need to know how much time it's going to take them to get there. The Weather Channel also added weather conditions near airports to help people know what they could expect if traveling by plane.

In addition to travelers, we discovered another group of weekend-oriented people who rely on information about the weather to inform their choice of outside activities. These folks have two questions: "Am I going to be able to do my activity?" and "If so, what do I need to wear?" It became clear to those planning programming that there was a timeframe involved. People wanted to know the weather the night before so that they could plan for their activities the next day.

Another group of Weather Channel watchers loves nature. They like to hear weather news from a specialist, like a horticulturalist, who could help them know what to do when it's time to plant flowers or fertilize.

Other people care about the weather only when it's disruptive—a thunderstorm, a hurricane, a snowstorm—anything that disrupts the flow of life. When severe weather kicks in, these people want to know that attention is being paid to the areas that are having severe weather—especially if it's their area. When severe weather hits certain parts of the country, those areas get much more exposure on The Weather Channel. That means putting reporters on the scene and experts in the studio that can give you all the information you need to know about the storm.

From a business perspective, implementing changes in programming based on real needs —both tangible and intangible—helped The Weather Channel become the market leader on TV and the Internet. Their profitability went from being in the lower third of the cable industry to the top five, because they knew exactly how to offer a portfolio of services to their different customer groups.

A cable channel that used to inform only "weather enthusiasts" became the weather authority that people trust for all the different ways weather affects life. ◆

Projects like The Weather Channel helped us understand that we could expand our research beyond product satisfaction and brand benefits. We realized that customers didn't just want to buy a product; they wanted a relationship (or a deeper connection) with the brands they valued in their lives. In response, we became focused on answering three questions:

Segments

What are the different groups of consumers a company wants to serve?

Needs

What needs are being met, not being met well or not being met at all?

Intangibles

How can my brand uniquely connect with the consumer both functionally and emotionally?

THE COMMITMENT MODEL BREAKTHROUGH

I left the product development world to do consulting so that I could delve more deeply into these questions across a wide range of consumer brands. I spent five years in strategic planning and new product creation for a consulting group that was on the leading edge of creating consumer surveys for long-range planning. Our in-depth questionnaires probed customers' needs, motivations, attitudes, purchase criteria, life circumstances and behaviors. We even shopped with consumers. Then we had research companies collect thousands of responses.

Sorting through all of this data for meaningful information required as much art as it did science. We were looking through the lens of human emotions as they related to product attributes and brand benefits, searching for the most important triggers for brand selection and loyalty. And we were also looking for ways to understand brand *segments*—so we wouldn't just understand what drove overall brand behavior, we would also be able to figure out which market segments offered the greatest opportunities. (See "Cleaning Up: A Case Study" on page 86 for a good example of this.)

In the mid-1990s, we hired John Copeland, a Ph.D. in social psychology with extensive modeling experience. Dr. Copeland quantitatively proved that understanding intangibles was critical to building higher levels of brand commitment, including:

We were looking through the lens of human emotions as they related to product attributes and brand benefits.

- *Loyalty*— **using only one brand of product or service**

- *Endorsement*— **willingness to endorse or advocate, like recommend to friend**

- *Influence*— **willingness to try new products or services from the same brand**

Eric Arnson | **Cleaning Up:** (**A Case Study**)

WHEN IT COMES TO INTRODUCING a new product, it's important to know what groups of people will be interested in using the product. The difficulty in consumer research is that there isn't just one consumer. In other words, you can't base your approach to consumers on the assumption that they are all the same. You need to segment customers into groups to see how similar or different they are.

When a business that produced cleaning products hired my company, our research discovered four segments of people:

- **I Want to Be Germ-Free:** Those who want a clean house for the sake of their health.

- **I'm Clean, Therefore I'm Good:** Those who want a clean house because they think they'll be judged by their peers.

- **I'll Try My Best:** Those who want a clean house but aren't fanatical about it.

- **It's My House:** Those who are fine with however their house looks.

So the question the cleaning company asked was this: If we're coming out with a new product that is the easiest new thing in cleaning, who among these four segments is the best target market? The Germ-Free clean freaks, right? Wrong. Unless you can show them that they will be able to get a microbe collection off the floor, they don't want what you have to offer. They want to be on their hands and knees scrubbing to kill germs.

How about the I'm Clean, Therefore I'm Good people—the ones who want to be neat and pristine because their friends are going to see their house? A seemingly obvious choice, but still wrong. They don't want a quick fix; they want to do a thorough job. They want their friends to be impressed with the amount of time and effort that went into cleaning the house.

Okay, does that mean we target the It's My House folks—the laziest people—because this product is so easy to use? Again, the answer is no. These people have stacks of stuff—and they like their stacks just where they are. That is their way. They aren't into clean, and it doesn't matter to them because there is something else that is more important for them to be doing with their time.

That leaves the I'll Try My Best group. And these people are the sweet spot for a new cleaning product. These people say, "Oh man, I'm not going to vacuum the whole house. But if I see a spill or I see something I want to clean up quickly, now there's an easier, quicker way to do it."

In this case, we used research to help us understand the different segments and to predict which segment would respond to the intangibles of the product. ◆

Effective brand management now required businesses to understand and nurture the emotional benefits and other brand intangibles of their products. Such consumer-based planning spread like wildfire throughout the packaged goods industry. As product managers and brand managers migrated into different industries (including durable goods, travel, financial services, insurance and retail), in-depth consumer-based planning quickly followed. Consumer data on emotions, motivations and attitudes—the intangibles that triggered increasing brand commitment—became a baseline requirement for effective strategic planning.

The breakthrough came when Dr. Copeland built a quantitative model that allowed us to narrow down the most significant intangible drivers of consumer commitment—a "Brand Commitment" model. He discovered that you could go into a product category, sort through statements about emotions, attitudes, motivations, etc. and then *empirically predict* the likelihood of any commitment level and the basis for commitment to your brand or a competitor's brand.

He expanded our earlier work on functional and emotional benefits to a broader view that includes a perspective on brand identity. *Who* is the brand, not just what products does it offer.

Consumer data on emotions, motivations and attitudes became a baseline requirement for effective strategic planning.

"Just Do It"

I can illustrate this with a simple, well-known consumer example. When you hear the word *Nike*, you may not immediately think of the product they sell. Instead, their slogan—"Just Do It"— could be the first thing that comes to mind. Nike's brand identity reflects this slogan, which is made of intangibles like its reputation, its personality and its history. Nike's brand identity can inspire you to try its products, but once you spend your money, those Nike shoes better deliver with great fit, great performance, great quality. You can make all the brand promises in the world (which is what brand identity is about), but unless you meet or exceed the expectations created by your promises, your product will fail. Meeting or exceeding expectations drives loyalty, word-of-mouth endorsements and recommendations—at the end of the day, brand commitment.

The beauty of the analysis . . .

The beauty of the analysis was that we could apply it across product categories. We looked at weather information. We looked at TV viewing. We looked at financial services. We looked at shoes. You name the category, and we applied the commitment model to it.

What the commitment model enabled us to do was to look at the "predictiveness" of someone trying a product . . . or not trying it. We could literally go into any given category and discover whether a person is likely to buy a lot or a little of a product.

The tricky part is that predictiveness hinges on understanding what's going on inside of people's hearts and minds. The measures we use are self-descriptive; we ask how strongly a consumer feels about things. We measure an emotion, an attitude or a motivation by measuring the strength of a response (*strongly agree, agree, disagree, strongly disagree,* etc.). Then we compare the response against other responses about desired benefits and behaviors to figure out what's really driving the consumer's behavior.

My colleagues and I have applied these principles and approaches to more than 250 brands in sixty categories. While most of these have been consumer goods and services, we have also pioneered new applications in the fields of leadership development and athletic training. We discovered that it doesn't appear to matter what the category is as long as it has functional dimensions and benefits, and emotional dimensions and benefits.

We wanted to use the commitment model to peer into the hearts of people.

GOOD FOR BUSINESS, AND GOOD FOR CHURCHES?

When this unique opportunity with Willow Creek Community Church arose, I was definitely intrigued with the notion of applying to the church world what we'd learned in the marketplace—and developing a greater understanding of how people grow spiritually.

We wanted to use the commitment model to peer into the hearts of people so we could understand what drives increasing love for God and increasing commitment to Christ. The challenge was incredible because this was completely new ground—an entire category that had never been explored from the inside out, so to speak.

We wanted to gain insight on the greatest opportunities for the church.

We wanted to discover what was most important—what worked (the "drivers") and what didn't work (the "barriers")—to create a growing level of commitment to Christ. We also wanted to know how satisfied people were with their spiritual growth, and how satisfied they were with the church's role in it. And we wanted to gain some insight on the greatest opportunities for the church: what else could the church offer—that they are not offering today—to help spiritual growth. For a category as complex as the Christian faith, we discovered the answers to these questions to be surprisingly simple, and extremely compelling.

Eric Arnson

appendix

REVEAL RESEARCH APPROACH AND METHODOLOGY

This project began with a simple question: Could scientific research help us understand and perhaps measure spiritual growth? I believed the answer was yes. I felt confident we could use the same research tools that measure attitudes and behaviors in consumers to measure spiritual beliefs and behaviors in individuals.

Here is a brief overview of our research approach and method.

APPROACH

Our approach focused on the three key areas and questions related to those areas:

- **Segments:** What are the different groups/segments of people the church might be looking to serve?

- **Needs:** What needs does each segment have that are being met, not being met well or not being met at all?

- **Drivers and Barriers:** What things are drivers of spiritual growth, and what things are barriers to spiritual growth?

These three areas provided the framework around which we organized the information we collected.

METHODOLOGY

Qualitative data helps clarify hypotheses, beliefs, attitudes and motivations.

Broadly speaking, there are two types of research methodology: qualitative and quantitative.

Qualitative

This is typically a one-on-one process in which a researcher poses questions directly to an individual. The questions often ask not only for information and opinions but also for the emotions and motivations behind those things. Researchers use qualitative data to help clarify hypotheses, beliefs, attitudes and motivations. Qualitative work is often a first step because it enables a researcher to fine-tune the language that will be used in quantitative tools.

Quantitative

This process utilizes detailed questionnaires distributed to thousands of people. Questions are typically multiple choice, and participants choose the most appropriate response among those listed for each question. Quantitative research collects a huge amount of data, which provides statisticians with a great deal of flexibility in analyzing results.

✦

We utilized both qualitative and quantitative methods in 2004 when we focused exclusively on Willow Creek Community Church. Here is a brief summary of the method used for the 2007 REVEAL research survey.

Qualitative Phase *(December 2006)*

- *One-on-one interviews with sixty-eight congregants.* We specifically recruited people in the more advanced stages of spiritual growth. Our goal was to capture language and insights to help guide the development of our survey questionnaire.

- *Interview duration: 30–45 minutes*

- *Focused on fifteen topics.* Topics included spiritual life history, church background, personal spiritual practices, spiritual attitudes and beliefs, etc.

Quantitative Phase *(January–February 2007)*

- E-mail survey fielded with seven geographically and culturally diverse churches

- Received 4,943 completed surveys, resulting in 1.4 million data points

- Utilized fifty-three sets of questions on topics such as:

Attitudes towards Christianity and one's personal spiritual life

Personal spiritual practices, including statements about frequency of Bible reading, prayer, journaling, solitude, etc.

Overall satisfaction with the church and specific church attributes

Most significant barriers to spiritual growth

Participation and satisfaction with church activities, such as weekend services, small groups, youth ministries and serving

✦

We used the highest research standards available, including a robust qualitative process.

In summary, we employed the highest research standards available, including a robust qualitative process. We also had a substantial number of respondents across a range of churches. Our analysis benefits greatly from such a strong response.

appendix  **3**

TWELVE BONUS DISCOVERIES

Discovery 1: Growing up in a church is the leading reason people begin to explore Christianity. Other reasons relate to personal feelings of emptiness or struggle.

The research shows there isn't much distinction across the spiritual continuum regarding how people begin their exploration of faith. This means that those who are in the Exploring Christianity segment and those who are in the Christ-Centered segment are equally likely to report they grew up in a church and so have known about Christianity all of their lives (see chart A3-1 on page 95).

Perhaps the most meaningful motivations—those that truly triggered a serious journey of spiritual exploration—are the four statements following "grew up in a church." These statements are largely unduplicated, which means these motivations are relatively independent. So people tended to pick "grew up in a church" and only one other motivation, not several. This means, for example, that while over 50 percent "grew up in a church," we believe that almost 30 percent began to seriously explore Christianity because "something was missing"; 20 percent were "looking for a higher purpose"; and 18 percent began their exploration due to "negative patterns," etc.

CHART A3-1

The Top Five Reasons
People Begin to Explore Christianity

Multiple responses were possible

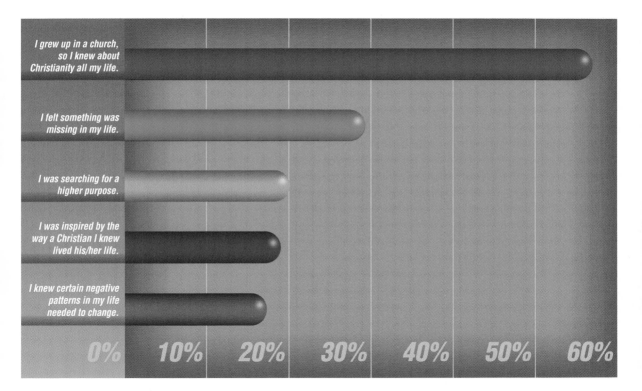

I grew up in a church, so I knew about Christianity all my life.

I felt something was missing in my life.

I was searching for a higher purpose.

I was inspired by the way a Christian I knew lived his/her life.

I knew certain negative patterns in my life needed to change.

0% 10% 20% 30% 40% 50% 60%

There are a few interesting minor differences along the spiritual continuum. For example, those in the Exploring Christianity and Growing in Christ segments are more likely than those in other segments to report that they are "searching for a higher purpose" and that "something is missing in my life."

Discovery 2: People begin attending their church primarily because of a personal relationship or recommendation.

The top three reasons people first come to a church are related to a personal relationship or recommendation. Other reasons include an intentional search for a local church or a visit triggered by curiosity.

CHART A3-2

The Top Five Reasons
People First Came to Their Church

Multiple responses were possible

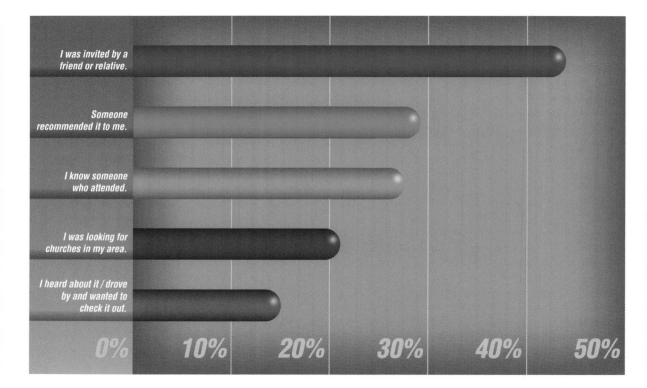

I was invited by a friend or relative.

Someone recommended it to me.

I know someone who attended.

I was looking for churches in my area.

I heard about it / drove by and wanted to check it out.

0% 10% 20% 30% 40% 50%

There is very little distinction across the spiritual continuum in how people find their church. Those in the Exploring Christianity and Growing in Christ segments are somewhat more likely to report that they were invited to church by a friend or relative.

Discovery 3: Expressions of gratitude toward God and dependence on God rise dramatically across the spiritual continuum.

The strength of people's feelings about their gratitude toward God and dependence on God more than double across the spiritual continuum.

Percentages specify those from each segment who "strongly agree" with each statement. For example, approximately 90 percent of all those in the Christ-Centered segment "strongly agreed" that "without God's help, I know I cannot make it on my own."

CHART A3-3

Feelings of Gratitude and Dependence on God Advance Strongly Across the Spiritual Continuum

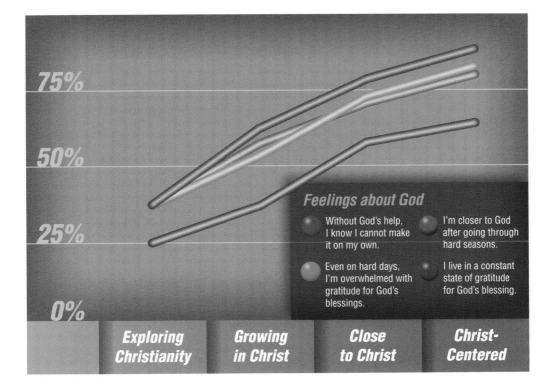

75%

50%

25%

0%

Feelings about God

- Without God's help, I know I cannot make it on my own.
- Even on hard days, I'm overwhelmed with gratitude for God's blessings.
- I'm closer to God after going through hard seasons.
- I live in a constant state of gratitude for God's blessing.

| *Exploring Christianity* | *Growing in Christ* | *Close to Christ* | *Christ-Centered* |

This is an excellent example of the types of statements we evaluated as we determined what was the most effective and predictive framework for understanding spiritual growth. The pattern of responses demonstrated on the chart reflects a strong alignment among multiple statements (about attitudes, behaviors, motivations, etc.) with the spiritual continuum. This kind of lockstep movement (as demonstrated in the chart above) means the accuracy and predictability of the segment framework is very high.

Discovery 4: People's feelings/attitudes about the importance of spiritual practices in their daily lives advance significantly along the spiritual continuum.

People's attitudes about the importance of prayer and Bible reading increase five to six times from the Exploring Christianity segment to the Christ-Centered segment.

Percentages specify those from each segment who "strongly agree" with each statement. For example, over 60 percent of all those in the Christ-Centered segment "strongly agreed" that "prayer is a central part of my daily life."

CHART A3-4

Attitudes about the Importance of Spiritual Practices Rise Dramatically Across the Spiritual Continuum

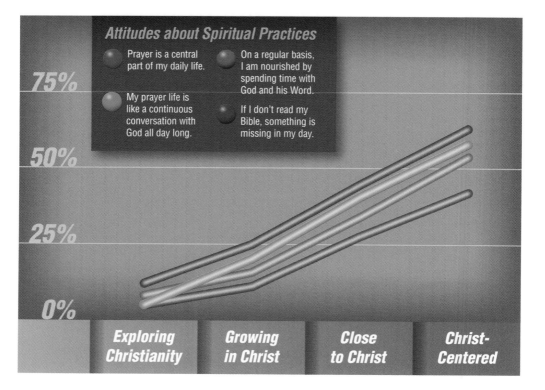

Attitudes about Spiritual Practices

- Prayer is a central part of my daily life.
- My prayer life is like a continuous conversation with God all day long.
- On a regular basis, I am nourished by spending time with God and his Word.
- If I don't read my Bible, something is missing in my day.

75%   50%   25%   0%

Exploring Christianity   Growing in Christ   Close to Christ   Christ-Centered

This chart shows that those who are in the Close to Christ and Christ-Centered segments aren't praying and reading the Bible with more regularity because they think they *should* or they *have to*. They engage in spiritual practices because they *want to*. Those who are farther along on the spiritual continuum anchor their relationship with Christ through a regular discipline of spiritual development. They place a high personal and emotional value on the role spiritual practices play in their lives.

Discovery 5: **People openly acknowledge that significant barriers, like addictions or emotional issues, impede their spiritual growth.**

Difficult issues often get in the way of people's spiritual growth. In general, the differences across the spiritual continuum are not noteworthy, with one exception.

CHART A3-5

Many Experience "Significant Barriers" to Spiritual Growth, Especially the Stalled Segment

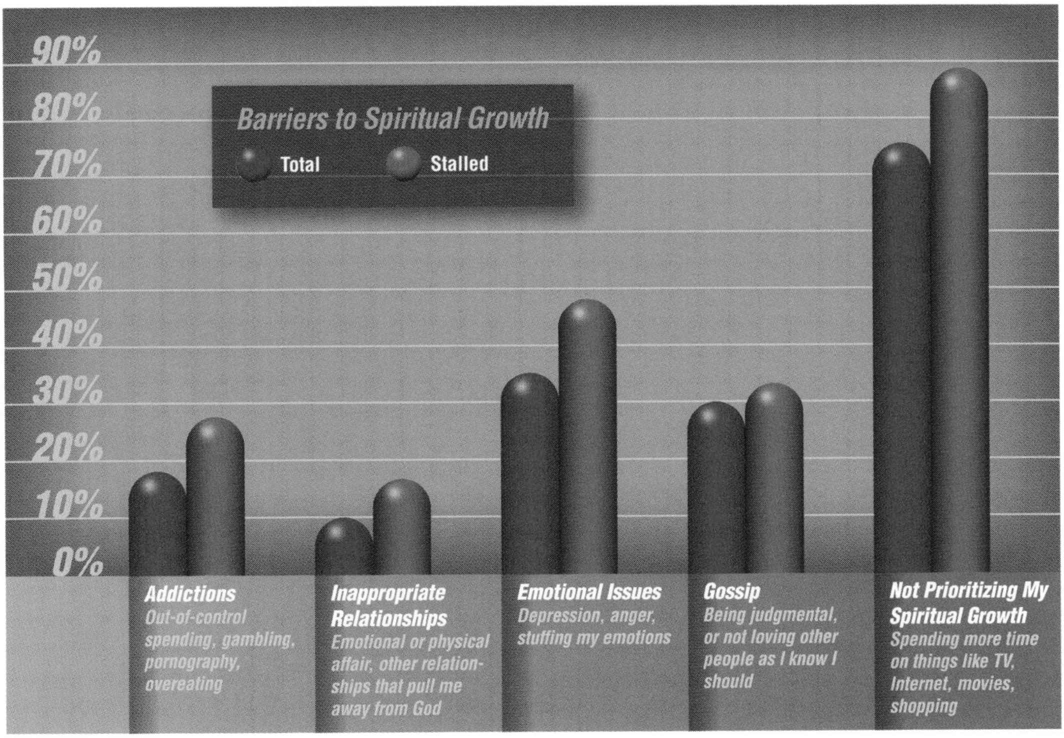

Barriers to Spiritual Growth

● Total ● Stalled

| **Addictions** Out-of-control spending, gambling, pornography, overeating | **Inappropriate Relationships** Emotional or physical affair, other relationships that pull me away from God | **Emotional Issues** Depression, anger, stuffing my emotions | **Gossip** Being judgmental, or not loving other people as I know I should | **Not Prioritizing My Spiritual Growth** Spending more time on things like TV, Internet, movies, shopping |

The Stalled segment stood out as the only segment on the spiritual continuum that consistently reported higher levels of "significant barriers" across all "barrier" categories (addictions, inappropriate relationships, etc.). It could be that these people came face-to-face with a life circumstance or personal challenge that threw them off track spiritually.

Discovery 6: As they advance along the spiritual continuum, people express a growing need for a spiritual community that "holds me accountable."

Spiritual relationships play an increasing role as people advance across the spiritual continuum. People also express an increasing need for these relationships to "hold me accountable" and "speak the truth to me."

Percentages specify those from each segment who "strongly agree" with each statement. For example, over 60 percent of all those in the Christ-Centered segment "strongly agreed" that "I have close relationships with other Christians who influence my life."

CHART A3-6

Attitudes about the Role and Importance of Spiritual Relationships Rise Across the Continuum

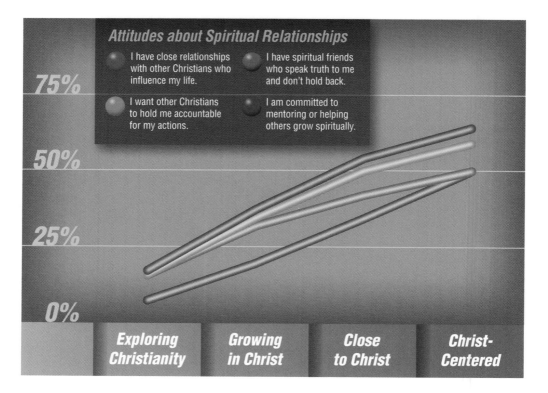

Attitudes about Spiritual Relationships

- I have close relationships with other Christians who influence my life.
- I have spiritual friends who speak truth to me and don't hold back.
- I want other Christians to hold me accountable for my actions.
- I am committed to mentoring or helping others grow spiritually.

75%
50%
25%
0%

| Exploring Christianity | Growing in Christ | Close to Christ | Christ-Centered |

Interestingly, the most advanced segments say they are committed to "mentoring or helping others grow spiritually"; 50 percent of the Christ-Centered segment "strongly agreed" with that statement.

Discovery 7: There are many reasons why people serve, but most importantly they feel it is an expression of their faith.

Attitudes about serving rise across the spiritual continuum. The chart below demonstrates an interesting hierarchy of reasons why people believe serving is important. Developing friendships appears to be much less important than other reasons, including "helping my church achieve its vision."

Percentages specify those from each segment who "strongly agree" with each statement. For example, over 75 percent of all those in the Christ-Centered segment "strongly agreed" that "serving is one of the most important expressions of being Christlike."

CHART A3-7

Why Do People Serve?

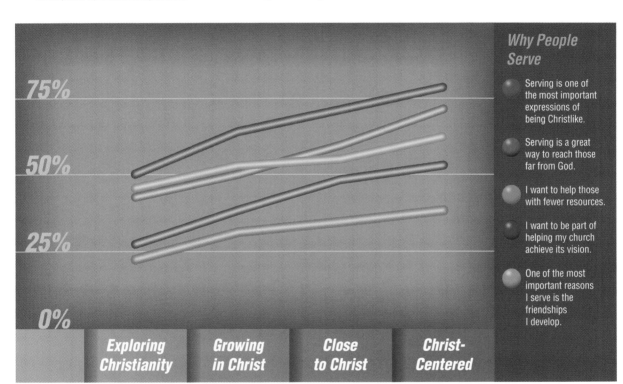

Another interesting observation is that, for the Close to Christ and Christ-Centered segments, "reaching those far from God" is the strongest motivation for serving after "it is the most important expression of being Christlike."

Discovery 8: The number one evangelistic activity for most segments is talking about prayer or offering to pray for non-Christians.

Survey respondents demonstrate an interesting mix of evangelistic activities, topped by either discussing prayer or offering to pray for non-Christians. All evangelistic activity increased along the spiritual continuum, confirming that our best evangelists are those who are in the later stages of spiritual growth.

CHART A3-8

Multiple responses were possible

The Top Five Evangelistic Activities

Talked about prayer or told them I'll pray for them

Invited them to church events / programs

Tried to learn more about their spiritual life

Gave them Christian books, music or message tapes / CDs

Talked meaningfully about non-church events (e.g. The Da Vinci Code movie)

0% 10% 20% 30% 40% 50% 60% 70%

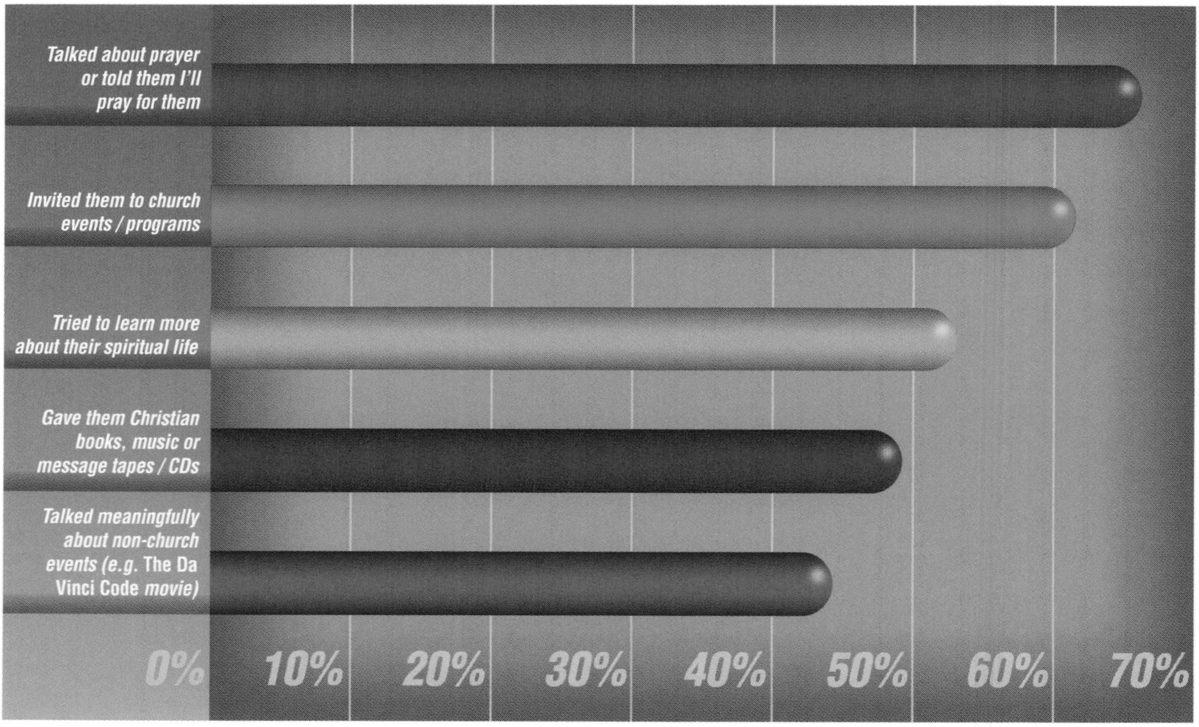

It's also interesting to observe that trying to "learn more about their spiritual life" drew slightly more responses than giving away Christian materials. Also, having conversations about non-church events, like movies, wasn't as significant as the other evangelistic activities.

Discovery 9: More than half of those surveyed said that they used the Internet at some point in the last year to advance their spiritual growth.

The chart below shows the percentage of people who used the Internet for five activities related to spiritual growth.

Percentages of all respondents who used the Internet in the last year for each activity. For example, approximately 55 percent of all respondents used the Internet at least once in the last year to "download services, messages or Christian music."

CHART A3-9

How Do People Use the Internet to Grow Spiritually?

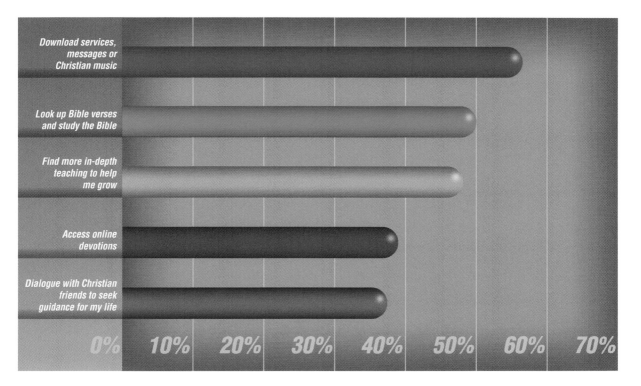

There isn't much distinction among the five activities, although it appears that downloading messages or music is the most popular option, and dialoguing with Christian friends is less common. There also wasn't much difference among segments across the spiritual continuum.

Discovery 10: **The Stalled and Dissatisfied segments are significantly more likely to say they are considering leaving their church.**

The chart below highlights the degree of unhappiness the Stalled and Dissatisfied segments feel toward their church by comparing their responses to "How long do you intend to stay at your church?" to the rest of the spiritual continuum.

CHART A3-10

Who Will Leave the Church?

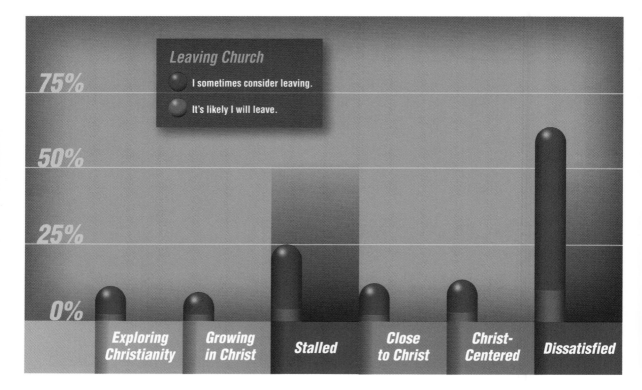

Leaving Church
- I sometimes consider leaving.
- It's likely I will leave.

75%

50%

25%

0%

Exploring Christianity | Growing in Christ | Stalled | Close to Christ | Christ-Centered | Dissatisfied

There is no definitive answer to why the Stalled and Dissatisfied segments are so disenchanted with the church they are attending. We believe the Stalled segment may be struggling with life circumstances or personal issues (see Discovery 5 on page 99). The Dissatisfied segment is full of sold-out Christ-followers who for some reason feel their current church is failing them. As we move ahead with our research, we plan to devote greater attention to discovering more about the Stalled and Dissatisfied segments.

Discovery 11: Six church attributes are most important to people, although satisfaction levels vary considerably.

We asked people about their satisfaction with thirty-five different church attributes. The six attributes shown on the chart below were most highly correlated with helping people grow spiritually.

Percentages of all respondents who said they were "very satisfied" with each church attribute. For example, over 70 percent of all respondents said they were "very satisfied" that their church "provides compelling worship services."

CHART A3-11

**Satisfaction with the
Top Six Church Attributes**

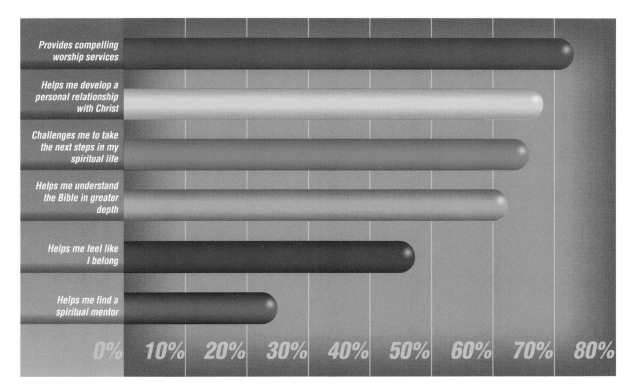

The research indicates a high level of satisfaction with weekend services and the spiritual development challenge provided by the church. Satisfaction is lower for two attributes related to providing spiritual community/relationships: "helps me feel like I belong" and "helps me find a spiritual mentor."

Discovery 12: People say weekend services are important to their spiritual growth, and they especially appreciate the singing/worship experience.

This chart demonstrates the importance people attach to weekend services, which most people (85 percent) attend three to four times a month.

Percentages of all respondents who said they "strongly agree" with each statement about weekend services at their church. For example, almost 70 percent of all respondents said they "strongly agreed" that "I make it (weekend service) a priority in my week."

CHART A3-12

What People Say about Weekend Services

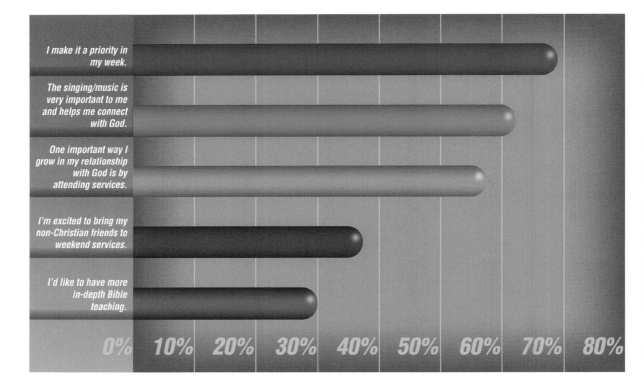

We do see some differences when we look at these attitudes across the spiritual continuum. The Christ-Centered segment is much more likely to be "excited to bring my non-Christian friends." The Dissatisfied segment is much more likely to want "more in-depth Bible teaching" and "more challenge" from the services.

| **Ministry Program** (Assessment Chart)

MINISTRY PROGRAM	EXPLORING CHRISTIANITY	GROWING IN CHRIST	CLOSE TO CHRIST	CHRIST-CENTERED

appendix **5**

CHARTS
AND ILLUSTRATIONS

ABOUT
THE AUTHORS

Greg L. Hawkins

Greg L. Hawkins is executive pastor of Willow Creek Community Church. Since 1996, he has assisted Senior Pastor Bill Hybels in providing strategic leadership to Willow Creek's five campuses and to the Willow Creek Association. He also serves as point leader for REVEAL, a new initiative within the WCA that utilizes research tools and discoveries to help churches better understand spiritual growth in their congregations. Prior to joining the staff of Willow Creek in 1991, Greg previously spent five years as a consultant for McKinsey & Company. He has an undergraduate degree in civil engineering from Texas A&M University and an MBA from Stanford University. Greg and his wife, Lynn, live in the Chicago suburbs with their three children.

Cally Parkinson

Cally Parkinson is brand manager for REVEAL, a new initiative within the WCA that utilizes research tools and discoveries to help churches better understand spiritual growth in their congregations. She previously served as the director of communication services at Willow Creek Community Church, a role she took on following a twenty-five-year career at Allstate Insurance Company. At Allstate, Cally held a number of different director- and officer-level positions in strategic planning, research, finance and communications. She has a BA in languages from Depauw University and a master's degree from the American Graduate School of International Management. Cally and her husband, Rich, live in the Chicago suburbs and have two grown children.

Eric Arnson

Eric Arnson is founder of ORIGINATE, a research and strategy consulting firm that develops and applies new approaches to understanding consumer-based loyalty. He also uses those consumer insights to help businesses create new products and services. Eric has over twenty-five years of experience in the brand and consumer strategy fields, serving mainly Fortune 500 companies. Previously, he served as a partner at McKinsey & Company, a partner at the Cambridge Group, and also as founder of ENVISION—a pioneer in consumer-driven brand strategy development. Eric began his career at Procter & Gamble before he moved on to Beecham Cosmetics. He is a graduate of the University of Michigan with a degree in literature, science and arts (LSA). Eric and his wife, Germaine, live in the Chicago area and have three children.

VISION, TRAINING, RESOURCES
FOR PREVAILING CHURCHES

This resource was created to serve you and to help you build a local church that prevails. It is just one of many ministry tools published by the Willow Creek Association.

The Willow Creek Association (WCA) was created in 1992 to serve a rapidly growing number of churches from across the denominational spectrum that are committed to helping unchurched people become fully devoted followers of Christ. Membership in the WCA now numbers over 12,000 churches worldwide from more than ninety denominations.

The Willow Creek Association links like-minded Christian leaders with each other and with strategic vision, training and resources in order to help them build prevailing churches designed to reach their redemptive potential. Here are some of the ways the WCA does that.

- **The Leadership Summit**—A once-a-year, two-and-a-half-day learning experience to envision and equip Christians with leadership gifts and responsibilities. Presented live on Willow Creek's campus as well as via satellite simulcast to over 135 locations across North America—plus more than eighty international cities via videocast—this event is designed to increase the leadership effectiveness of pastors, ministry staff, volunteer church leaders and Christians in the marketplace.

- **Ministry-Specific Conferences**—Throughout the year the WCA hosts a variety of conferences and training events—both at Willow Creek's main campus and offsite, across North America and around the world. These events are for church leaders and volunteers in areas such as group life, children's ministry, student ministry, preaching and teaching, the arts and stewardship.

- **Willow Creek Resources®**—Provides churches with trusted and field-tested ministry resources on important topics in areas such as leadership, volunteer ministries, spiritual formation, stewardship, evangelism, group life, children's ministry, student ministry, the arts and more.

- **WCA Member Benefits**—Includes substantial discounts to WCA training events, a 20 percent discount on all Willow Creek Resources®, *Defining Moments* monthly audio journal for leaders, quarterly *Willow* magazine, access to a Members-Only section on the WCA website, monthly communications and more. Member Churches also receive special discounts and premier services through the WCA's growing number of ministry partners—Select Service Providers—and save an average of $500 annually depending on the level of engagement.

For specific information about WCA conferences, resources, membership and other ministry services contact:

WILLOW

Willow Creek Association
P.O. Box 3188 • Barrington, IL 60011-3188 • Phone: 847–570–9812 • Fax: 847–765–5046
www.willowcreek.com

WILLOW
Willow Creek Resources